W9-AHC-714

Perspectives on
PSYCHOLOGY
and the MEDIA

Edited by
Sam Kirschner
Diana Adile Kirschner

AMERICAN PSYCHOLOGICAL ASSOCIATION

WASHINGTON, DC

Published by
American Psychological Association
750 First Street, NE
Washington, DC 20002

Copies may be ordered from
American Psychological Association
Order Department
P.O. Box 92984
Washington, DC 20090-2984

In the UK and Europe, copies may be ordered from
American Psychological Association
3 Henrietta Street
Covent Garden, London
WC2E 8LU England

Typeset in Palatino by Innodata Publishing Services, Halethorpe, MD

Printer: Kirby Lithographic Company, Inc., Arlington, VA
Cover Designer: Minker Design, Bethesda, MD
Technical/Production Editor: Catherine R. Worth

Library of Congress Cataloging-in-Publication Data

Perspectives on Psychology and the Media / edited by Sam Kirschner, Diana
    Adile Kirschner. — 1st ed.
        p.   cm. — (Psychology and the media ; 1)
    Includes bibliographical references and index.
    ISBN 1–55798–433–6 (acid free paper)
    1. Mass media—Psychological aspects.   I. Kirschner, Sam, 1948–
        II. Kirshner, Diana Adile, 194–.   III. Series.
    P96.P75P47   1997
    302.23'01'9–dc21   97-5538
                                                                                        CIP

British Library Cataloguing-in-Publication Data
A CIP record is available from the British Library

Printed in the United States of America
First edition

Contents

Research

Practice

Epilogue

Contributors

Edward Donnerstein, Department of Communications, University of California, Santa Barbara

Norma Deitch Feshback, Department of Psychology, University of California, Los Angeles

Seymour Feshback, Department of Psychology, University of California, Los Angeles

Lilli Friedland, Private Practice, Los Angeles

George Gerbner, Dean Emeritus, The Annenberg School for Communication, University of Pennsylvania

E. Ann Kaplan, Humanities Institute, State University of New York, Stony Brook

Florence W. Kaslow, Director, Florida Couples and Family Institute, West Palm Beach; Visiting Professor of Psychology, Florida Institute of Technology; Visiting Professor of Medical Psychiatry, Duke University Medical Center

Diana Adile Kirschner, Private Practice, Gwynedd Valley, Pennsylvania

Sam Kirschner, Private Practice, Gwynedd Valley, Pennsylvania

Fredrick Koenig, Department of Sociology, Tulane University, New Orleans

Lawrence Kutner, Kutner & Olson, Inc., Lafayette, California, and Department of Psychiatry, Harvard Medical School

Stacy L. Smith, Department of Communications, University of California, Santa Barbara

Richard Tanenbaum, Private Practice, Bethesda, Maryland

Foreword

The advent of this volume heralds the evolution of media psychology into a recognized specialty area of practice in psychology. The fact that it is being published by the American Psychological Association (APA) indicates the growing esteem in which psychologists who work with the media are held within the profession, as well as within the communications industry. It has been a precarious and turbulent journey prior to our arrival at this juncture; in the early years those working with and in media were often criticized and rebuked. The ambivalent reactions to psychologists' involvement in media are discussed and amply documented in the preface and in chapter 5, "The Pioneers of Media Psychology." Clearly these pioneers initially met with less than rave reviews from their professional colleagues. This state of affairs has completely turned around as APA has come to understand the importance of the media. For example, in 1995, the APA Public Information Office launched a massive public education campaign designed to promote the image of psychology.

The Division of Media Psychology (Division 46) celebrated its 10th anniversary at the 105th annual APA Convention in Toronto in August, 1996. Nine of the division's ten illustrious past presidents presented their reminiscences, trials and tribulations, and hopes for the future of the field. It is a profession that continues to expand rapidly, fueled in part by the explosion in new technological advances like the Internet, e-mail, and virtual reality. In fact, the Division recently decided to add the words "and communications technology" to its name. Much of the ferment of the past decade is reflected in the chapters of this book.

The editors, Drs. Sam and Diana Kirschner, have sought to encompass the breadth of the field by inviting papers on both research and practice, because media psychologists engage in both, and each aspect is complementary to the other. The four chapters in the research section focus primarily on television, highlighting images conveyed in various programs and their influence on viewers, particularly the impact of violence and of overt sexuality on those who are watching and listening. These chapters emphasize how important it is for media psychologists to base their on-air and written comments on factual evidence and not on personal opinion. It is critical that media psychologists be conversant with the scientific data regarding topics for which their expertise is sought and that they do not go beyond the data to please a talk show host or news room director.

Some of the roles psychologists undertake and fulfill in the media are described and discussed in the practice section. These include roles in international radio, newsprint, television, and film. There are certainly additional arenas in which we function, and it is anticipated that these will be covered in subsequent volumes in this series. What is contained in the practice section provides a colorful smorgasbord of current happenings written by seasoned professionals who deal with the media daily.

All that media psychologists do should occur within the context of the principles established in the APA Ethical Principles and Code of Conduct along with other pertinent standards of practice. At the time of this writing, proposed APA guidelines for media psychologists are currently wending their way through the APA governance.

We believe the publication of this volume marks a felicitous and important occasion. The chapters included herein will become part of a new, emergent body of literature that begins to fill a gap in the knowledge base for all of those interested in communication and psychological practice in and through the media.

Florence W. Kaslow

Preface

Media psychology has evolved into an important and respected field in psychology. It encompasses a multiplicity of diverse activities, including but not limited to interpreting psychological findings for a nonprofessional audience by appearing on radio and television shows as guests or hosts, consulting to the print media and television, writing for newspapers and magazines, and conducting research on the impact of television on viewers.

There was a time, however, when the profession of psychology did not look favorably upon those who participated in the media. The ethics of the early pioneers of media psychology were strongly questioned. But in the 1970s and 1980s psychologists were forced to contend with the enormous popularity of call-in radio and television programs that regularly included psychologists as guests and hosts. As a result, leading psychologists began to organize themselves into a professional organization that would focus on the role of mental health professionals in the media.

In 1982, a group of mental health professionals came together to form the Association of Media Psychology (AMP). Jacqueline Bouhoutsos, AMP's founder and a clinical psychologist, was involved in conducting research and writing about ethical issues for psychologists. She was also a member of the motion picture rating board, which may have led to her interest in the area of media psychology. The first official meeting was held at the California State Psychological Association (CSPA) meeting in San Diego, in March of 1982. This meeting was attended by a group of psychologists including Jacqueline Bouhoutsos, who not only was founder of AMP but also past-president of CSPA; Jerry Clark; Toni Grant, a well-known talk show host and psychologist; Mae Ziskin, president of CSPA; Fred Koenig (New Orleans); Michael Mantell (San Diego); Michael Broder (Philadelphia); Larry McCauly (Oklahoma); Elliott Wiener (Portland); Diane Cole (Orange County); Karen Blaker (New York); Diane Hull (Santa Barbara); Bob McCall (Philadelphia); Stu Fishchoff (Los Angeles); and Steve Brody (Cambria).

At the time, most of the people involved in AMP were doing radio or TV call-in shows. Others wrote for the print media or functioned as

experts for the broadcast media. For example, Fred Koenig was presenting behavioral science news on a local radio station, and Bob
McCall wrote for newspapers as well as worked as a regular columnist,
contributing editor, and feature writer for *Parents Magazine*. The atten-
dees brought out the videotapes and audiotapes from their shows and
got feedback from their colleagues. Unfortunately, many of the "stars"
in media psychology, that is, the psychologists who were either on the
air or in print, and who had the biggest audiences, did not participate
in this association.

AMP's mission was to promote the participation of psychologists
and mental health professionals in the media, to formulate ethical and
professional standards for media involvement, and to educate the public through the media. AMP had its own officers and created its own
ethical guidelines. A committee, chaired by Michael Broder, formu-
lated the first AMP guidelines for media psychologists. In the fall of
1983, a meeting was held in San Francisco where the first formal program was developed for the 1984 APA convention in Los Angeles.

At the APA convention in Toronto in 1985, AMP members asked for
information from APA as to the requirements for becoming a division.
An APA representative met with AMP members and described the
requirements and the process. The membership went about the difficult task of getting the necessary signatures. This was particularly
demanding because many APA members believed that there were
already too many divisions. Jackie Bouhoutsos and Jerry Clark button-
holed, cajoled, and persuaded members to get signatures on the peti-
tions and get members of APA governance to vote to establish a new
division of media psychology.

Division 46 came into being in 1985, with Jacqueline Bouhoutsos as
the first President. Fred Koenig was first editor of the newsletter, the
AMPplifier. Since then, the Division has encouraged its members to
conduct research and to practice media psychology within strict ethical
guidelines. The Public Information Committee of APA and Division 46
have recently drafted a proposed set of ethical guidelines for psychologists in the media that are currently undergoing the APA review
process.

Media psychology has also received attention from the leaders of
APA. For example, George Miller, in his presidential address, called
upon psychologists to "give psychology away" because psychologists
have expertise that the community could use. William Bevin, another
APA president, suggested in his presidential address that psycholo-

gists communicate to broader audiences because "altruism is the most enlightened self-interest." He felt that the act of giving psychological information to the broad public would make psychology more relevant and would gain the public's support for psychology. Since the time of these APA leaders, nearly every candidate for APA's presidency has suggested that psychologists communicate more extensively with the public.

Media psychology is a field that has come of age. In recognition of the enormous role that psychologists play in their media work, Division 46 and APA Books have launched a series of volumes dedicated to the field of media psychology. This book is the first volume in that series. *Perspectives on Psychology and the Media* has brought together some of the leading professionals in the field. They include the foremost researchers, pioneers, and practitioners of the art.

The coeditors would like to acknowledge Florence Kaslow, past-president of Division 46 and chair of its Publications Board, who spearheaded the effort to create this book series and will serve as its general editor. Dr. Kaslow, an accomplished media psychologist, has also contributed to this volume.

Lilli Friedland
Diana Kirschner
Sam Kirschner

Research

1

Children's Empathy and the Media: Realizing the Potential of Television

Norma Deitch Feshbach and Seymour Feshbach

The role of television in the lives of America's children has occupied the interest of scholars since the very inception of the medium. It has also become an issue of major public concern, even entering the political arena. The principal source of this concern has been the depiction of violence on television. Other program contents to which objections have been voiced are sexual themes and the portrayal of family structures that deviate from the traditional family paradigm.

The contemporary thrust of public policy in response to these concerns has been the implementation of mechanisms such as the "V-chip" that can provide parents better control of the programs that their children view. It is uncertain whether this approach will prove to be effective in protecting children from observing content that parents and the community believe to be undesirable and harmful. However, even if the use of the V-chip is reasonably successful, this approach to the management of television in the lives of children will remain inadequate.

Preventing children from viewing programs that are deemed undesirable is a negative action that conveys little about the type of programming that is desirable. It is somewhat analogous to the use of punishment for "bad" behavior without teaching the child what is "good" behavior. The issue of television programming and children should not be framed solely in terms of the content that children should not view. Television is a medium that can function as a rich source of constructive knowledge for children. For example, television can depict the manifold ways in which ethnic diversity enriches our culture. It can portray the many roles and opportunities that are available to young people, regardless of gender. TV can also present images of cooperation and nonviolent resolutions of conflict. We are not suggesting that television content should merely depict prosocial themes. What we are suggesting is that television can play an important role in enlarging the horizons of children and that public policy should encourage the realization of this potential.

A key element in actualizing television's educational potential is the role played by the child's capacity for empathy. Empathy facilitates, and in some circumstances makes possible, social understanding and social communication. It has a dual relation to television. Empathy is a psychological mechanism that mediates a child's understanding of and emotional response to television. It is also a cognitive and emotional process that can be influenced and enhanced by television viewing. In this chapter we will focus on the place and role of empathy in the interaction between the child and the television medium.

Empathy and the Dramatic Experience

The human capacity for empathy plays a significant part in the response to the dramatic content of theater, film, and television. The history of human interest in and response to dramatic presentation is almost as old as the history of human civilization itself. Theater, in one form or another, has long held a fascination for young and old audiences from diverse cultures. With the advent of cinema and then of television, the size of the audience and the frequency with which it is exposed to dramatic presentations has increased enormously. Knowledge of the processes that mediate audience involvement in dramatic presentations and determine their attraction, and of the psychological effects of repeated and prolonged exposure to these media stimuli, is clearly important from a pragmatic as well as a theoretical perspective.

One of the striking and puzzling features of media involvement is the "as-if" nature of the audience response to drama. The audience often reacts to dramatic presentations as if they were real, even though they may at the same time know that the depicted events are fictional. Despite the fictional nature of the dramatic stimuli, viewers react with real sadness, fear, joy, anger, or pride. Dramatic presentations can elicit the full gamut of human emotional responses that are generally reserved for significant, meaningful real life experiences. To what extent are the mechanisms mediating responses to drama similar to those mediating responses to real life events?

In addressing this question, one should take into account two major apparent differences between drama and real life: (a) the events or drama are being enacted and are not real; (b) the events or drama that elicit emotions in the viewer are happening to someone else but in real life the events are happening to the viewer. With regard to this second distinction, the viewer sometimes behaves as if he or she were the direct object of the affect eliciting event. Further blurring this distinction between the experience of drama and the experience of real life is the observation that an emotion arousing event occurring to another person will frequently elicit a similar feeling in an observer. This process of emotions elicited in adults and children through the vicarious sharing of the affect experienced by the person is called empathy.

A 4-year-old, saddened by observing the distress of another child who has just fallen off a bicycle, is displaying empathy; the camper who responds with anxiety as he observes the fear of a camp-mate who has been inadvertently trapped on an isolated rock ledge during a mountain climb is also displaying empathy, as is the child who experiences happiness in response to the joy manifested by a "birthday" child as the latter opens each birthday present. These empathic behaviors bear a striking similarity, at least on a superficial level, to the distress, even tears, experienced by a television viewer who observes on the screen the grief of a child who is being separated from a sick parent, to the dread the viewer feels as he or she observes the fright of a child cowering in the darkness to avoid being discovered by a dangerous assailant, and to the smiles and joy that can be seen on viewers' faces as their favorite television hero triumphs over the villain and is awarded knighthood and treasures by a grateful king.

Clearly there are analogies between children's emotional responses to the experiences of fantasy characters they observe on television—and on films and in the theater—and their emotional responses to the experiences of real people with whom they interact in their daily lives. However, there are perils in assuming equivalence on the basis of analogy. A primary question to which this chapter is addressed is whether the process of empathy is a critical element in the transaction between the televised drama and the television viewer. Further analysis and understanding of the process mediating viewers' affective responses to fantasy events and the experience of empathy in real life may reveal important points of difference as well as similarity.

There may well be a reciprocal relationship between the child and television such that under certain conditions empathy mediates the child's affective response to television and under other conditions particular kinds of emotional interaction on television foster the development of empathy in the child viewer. There is empirical evidence that television viewing can enhance certain cognitive competencies, stimulate social behaviors, and evoke a range of emotional reactions (Collins, 1982; Dorr, 1982; Huston et al., 1992). To the extent that these competencies, behaviors, and reactions are implicated in empathic behavior, exposure to relevant programming on television should enhance empathy in children.

This latter possibility, namely the potential role of television in the development and enhancement of children's empathy, is important from a social as well as a theoretical perspective. Empathy, in addition to being an interesting psychological process and phenomenon, has been shown to be related to positive, prosocial behaviors. The child high in empathy is likely to be less aggressive, more cooperative, and more generous than the child low in empathy (Eisenberg & Fabes, 1990; Eisenberg & Miller, 1987; Feshbach, 1978; Feshbach & Feshbach, 1982). There is also evidence that empathy facilitates a positive self-concept (Feshbach & Feshbach, 1982). Empathy, then, may prove to be a significant mediating mechanism through which particular dramatic presentations in the media can be utilized to foster personal development and positive social behaviors.

The process of empathy itself requires considerable clarification, however. There are different levels of empathy that derive from the complexity of cognitive elements entailed in the empathic process and the refinement of the affective response, and there are alternate views and theoretical models of empathy. Some may have more bearing than others on the television experience. There are also significant individual differences in empathic responsiveness; an examination of these differences, in addition to refining our understanding of empathy, may also bear on individual differences in emotional responses to dramatic presentations and in empathic development stimulated by television dramas.

Thus, before addressing the question of the role of empathy in children's responses to television, a brief review of pertinent psychological literature on empathy will be presented. Theoretical treatments of empathy and relevant research data will be reviewed. Next, the question of the possible role of empathy in children's emotional responses to television will be addressed. The question of the possible effects of television on the development of empathy in children will then be considered. In addition, in the course of discussing these issues, the relationship between empathy and fantasy will be examined.

Empathy in Children

Historical Notes

Empathy is generally considered to play a major role in the social development of an individual. However, there is less consensus with regard to conceptions of empathy, its functions, its antecedents, its optimal assessment procedures, and its role in the evolutionary survival of a species. Prior to the 1970s there were only sporadic efforts to evaluate systematically some of these controversial issues. Then, during the seventies, a considerable expansion occurred of research on issues relevant to children's empathy. Paradoxically, given the potential intrinsic relationship between television and empathy, only a few studies simultaneously and directly investigated these dual topics.

At the turn of the century, Theodore Lipps, a German psychologist, referred to the phenomenon of *einfuhling*, the literal translation of which is "feeling into another." *Einfuhling* described the process by which an observer takes on the emotion and "motor attitudes" of another person as reflected in the responses of spectators to performances of others and even to the appreciation of the emotions conveyed in a work of art (Lipps, 1906). Of note is the emphasis given to the vicarious sharing of an affective experience, an emphasis that continues to be represented in several contemporary multidimensional approaches to the study of empathy. Although there are a number of different versions of such affective approaches to empathy, the requirement of an affective correspondence between the emotional experience of the observer and the observed is critical for distinguishing the affective approaches to empathy from those approaches employing predominantly cognitive criteria

(Davis, 1983c; Feshbach, 1975; Hoffman, 1982a; McDougall, 1960; Sullivan, 1953; Zahn-Waxler & Radke-Yarrow, 1982). This correspondence requires some degree of specificity in that the empathic observer feels fear when the observed experiences a threat rather than the observer reporting a general dysphoric reaction to these particular emotional states in the observed.

An early formulation of empathy in predominantly cognitive terms appeared in the writings of George Herbert Mead (1974). A critical element in his theorizing was the acquisition of social empathy through role-taking and imitation. For Mead, empathy facilitated social interaction, because through this process a person could anticipate another's actions and be ready with an appropriate response. The context of play in which the child behaves in an "as-if" manner is where the cause and effect factors of social interaction and transactions are learned. Although Mead suggested that empathy involved feeling as well as thinking, it was the latter component that was predominant in his conceptualizations of the term. Mead's attention to the activity of role-taking anticipated an essential feature of cognitive definitions and explanations of the phenomenon of empathy. His account was also conducive to the construction of the empathic process as a mechanism for predicting the attitudes and behaviors of other people.

Contemporary Perspectives

During the 1970s the nature of the internal response in the empathic process, whether cognitive or affective, was the subject of much theoretical debate and difference. Subsequently, this debate has subsided and there appears to be a general consensus that empathy entails both affective and cognitive elements, the relative role of each varying with the situation and the age and personality of the child (Feshbach, 1978, 1982; Eisenberg & Fabes, 1990; Hoffman, 1975, 1977, 1982a). According to N. Feshbach, although empathy is defined as a shared emotional response between observer and stimulus person, it is contingent upon cognitive factors. In this integrative–affective model, the affective empathy reaction is postulated to be a function of three component factors: (a) the cognitive ability to discriminate affective cues in others, (b) the cognitive skill to assume the perspective and role of another person, and (c) the affective ability to experience emotions (Feshbach, 1975, 1978; Feshbach & Kuchenbecker, 1974). Implicit in this and other models of empathy is the critical requirement of differentiation of self from object.

There are instances of strong identifications and lack of separateness in which the observer's affective reactions appear to be primarily self-oriented rather than a reflection of genuine empathy. When one feels dejected because the home team has lost a critical game, is it because of empathy for the players' loss or is one primarily reacting to one's own loss? Either or both can be the case. The point here is the relevance of the distinction with regard to empathy. One can feel badly because one believes that the players are very disappointed and upset, and one can vicariously share their experience. One can also feel badly because the defeat of one's team denotes, to some degree, a personal defeat. One may experience a loss of status, a lowering of self-esteem; that is, one's own sense of well-being, one's self-concept is in some sense contingent upon the success or failure of one's team (or school, or ethnic group, or nation).

Hoffman's developmental model also has three components—cognitive, affective, and motivational—and focuses on empathic responses to distress in others as the motivation for altruistic behaviors (1977, 1982a, 1982b). For Hoffman, empathic arousal is already reflected in infant behavior such as infant cries in response to peer crying (Simner, 1971), and he ascribes reflexive and innate origins to the emergence of empathy (Sagi & Hoffman, 1976). Empathic behavior subsequently becomes transformed when the cognitive system of the child develops (Hoffman, 1977). Although socialization influences are acknowledged by Hoffman to shape empathic responding, biological predispositional propensities are afforded a strong role. Further, even behaviors such as emotional contagion are included under the general rubric of empathy.

These varied conceptions of empathy have implications beyond academic distinctions. Each of these conceptions of empathy relate to different psychological processes that have different psychological implications with regard to the child's response to television content.

Ontogeny of Empathy

The most impressive empirical support for the early emergence of empathy is reflected in the studies carried out by Zahn-Waxler and Radke-Yarrow (1982). In their studies very young children exhibited "empathy-like" behaviors. We refer to these behaviors as "empathy like" because many of the behaviors exhibited by the toddlers could easily be categorized as altruistic and helpful. There appears to be a close theoretical and empirical relationship between empathy and prosocial behavior (Feshbach, 1982, 1983; Feshbach & Feshbach, 1986). Nevertheless, in our view, empathy, while related to other social behaviors, is distinct and not synonymous with helping, caring, and sharing. Thus, once again the position one takes about the ontogeny of empathy depends to some extent on one's theoretical concept of empathy.

There is, however, considerable evidence of age-related changes in the components mediating empathy. The cognitive demands of perspective taking vary markedly in complexity. A preschooler may have some understanding of the feelings and perspective of another child whose favorite toy has been broken but will not yet comprehend the work situation of a parent who has been denied a merited advancement. Studies of children's understanding of emotions depicted in television cartoons indicate that the ability to identify the emotions depicted by the cartoon characters varies with the age of the child (Knowles & Dixon, 1990). Some emotions such as jealousy, readily comprehended by adults, are difficult for 6- and 8-year-olds to identify. Nevertheless, children do experience vicarious emotions in response to both factual and fictional people they observe on television (Huston, Wright, Alvarez, & Truglio, 1995).

In general, children, at a very early age discriminate emotional signs in others. Empathy emerges early but becomes more differentiated and purposeful with additional years. Finally, not all children are equally responsive or equally empathic, nor do all situations have equal salience for eliciting empathy.

In addition to attributes of the child, such as age and cognitive level, that influence empathy, attributes of the stimulus situation also influence empathy. Thus similarity between the observer and the individual observed has been found to increase empathic behavior in both adults and children (Feshbach, 1978; Stotland & Dunn, 1963).

Empathic and Prosocial Behavior

We have said that empathy is not identical to prosocial behavior. The need for this important theoretical and empirical distinction relates to whether empathy invariably serves as the motivation for altruistic behavior. Prosocial behaviors, especially altruism, can be mediated by factors other than empathy such as modeling and reinforcement. Conversely, when empathy is aroused, altruistic behavior does not inevitably follow (Feshbach, 1982).

Although extant research findings generally reflect a positive relationship between empathy and prosocial behavior, the direction and strength of the findings vary as a function of the manner in which empathy is defined and measured and on the specific prosocial behavior being evaluated (Eisenberg & Miller, 1987; Feshbach, 1982; Feshbach & Feshbach, 1986). In like manner, a number of studies report an inverse relationship between empathy and aggression across a wide age range and through use of a variety of assessment techniques (Feshbach, 1983; Feshbach & Feshbach, 1982; Mehrabian & Epstein, 1972; Rothenberg, 1970).

The observed inverse association between empathy and antisocial behavior led to a series of training studies in which a curriculum based on the three-component model of empathy was developed and implemented with elementary school children for the purpose of regulating aggression and promoting prosocial behaviors (Feshbach, 1979, 1983, 1984; Feshbach, Feshbach, Fauvre, & Ballard-Campbell, 1983). In general, the findings from this program indicated that engaging in empathy training resulted in reduced aggressive behaviors and enhanced self-esteem as well as increased prosocial behaviors. These findings provide alternative methodological support for the positive relationship between empathy and prosocial behavior that has been obtained in correlational studies. In addition, the findings indicate that empathy, although an individual difference trait, is also malleable. The study also delineates the processes that may be implicated in empathic behavior. It is possible that some of these same processes can be stimulated and enhanced through particular film and television programming.

In these training programs children participated in exercises and activities that focused on discrimination of relevant affective cues, cognitive perspective and role taking skills, and affect related exercises. They did not participate in exercises that directly addressed aggressive behaviors or alternatives to aggression. Yet, at the conclusion of the 30 hours of training, the children who participated in the empathy training program exhibited less aggressive behavior and more prosocial behavior in their classroom interactions.

The pattern of correlations obtained in the study was generally consistent with the experimental findings. Children high in empathy tended to manifest more prosocial behavior and related cognitive competencies than children low in empathy. There were some sex differences in the pattern of these correlations, with cognitive correlates such as social comprehension, reading, and vocabulary skills being more pronounced for boys than for girls and correlations with prosocial behavior and self-concept being more pronounced for girls than for boys.

The assessment of empathy in this case was based on a set of short videotapes (Feshbach, 1982). An earlier measure, the Feshbach and Roe (1968) Situation Test of Empathy (FASTE), developed in our laboratory at UCLA, has been used extensively with preschool through elementary school age children (Hoffman, 1982b; Radke-Yarrow, Zahn-Waxler, & Chapman, 1983). The measure consists of a series of slide sequences in which children the same age and sex as the subject are shown in different affect-eliciting situations (e.g., the child has lost a pet dog). Accompanying each sequence is a short narration that describes the events depicted in the slides. After observing a slide sequence, the child is asked, "How do you feel?" In order for empathy to be scored, the child's response must reflect a correspondence between reported and depicted affect.

The subsequent measure for use with latency age children (Feshbach, 1982) that was employed in the empathy training study consists of a series of 2- to 2 ½-minute videotapes showing real children involved in common childhood emotion evoking situations. In each videotape, a story character is shown within an affect-laden situation where his or her immediate facial, postural, behavioral, and verbal emotional reactions are displayed. The emotions of pride and happiness were designated as euphoric empathy; the emotions of anger, fear, and sadness as dysphoric. Separate sets of 10 visual-audio tapes have been developed for boys and girls with story characters of the same sex as the subjects. In general, each videotaped story builds to an emotionally intense climax. At the end of each tape, the viewing child is asked to indicate what he or she is feeling and to rate the intensity of that feeling.

These measures have been described in some detail because of their correspondence to the television–child interaction. The video sequences are analogous to a television drama, and the child's affective responses to the brief video sequences are analogous to the child's affective responses to dramatic sequences on television. This similarity between the situation entailed in the measure and that entailed in television facilitates generalization of studies using this measure to the child's empathic responses to television content.

The Role of Empathy in the Response to Dramatic Presentations

We turn now to a consideration of the role of empathy in mediating children's reactions to dramatic presentations, especially those on television. Children display a variety of emotional reactions when viewing television. They cover their eyes, they giggle, they cry, they jump up and down, they recoil, they scream, they bite their nails, and they smile and laugh. When these feelings correspond to those of the television characters they are observing, the child may be displaying empathy.

The human capacity for empathy is an important constituent in the response to media as it is in everyday social interaction. The cognitive component of perspective and role-taking enables the viewer to understand the motivations and feelings of the characters in a drama or in a documentary. It helps the viewer appreciate the characters' perceptions of the situations that confront them and the choices they make, stemming from these perceptions. Of course, one can understand and respond to the verbal and physical actions observed on television without being cognizant of or concerned with the motives, perspectives, and feelings of the protagonists. Preschoolers do not need empathy to be engaged and entertained by Saturday morning cartoon fare. Indeed, there are adult action programs that require little in the way of empathic understanding and feeling on the part of the audience to be comprehensible to and involve the viewer.

Nevertheless, most programs that are judged to be imaginative, aesthetic, and of high quality, whether directed toward the elementary school age or adult audience, require audience empathy in order to be fully understood and experienced. Viewer empathy is demanded by programs that attempt to convey an inner conflict of a protagonist or a conflict between two reasonable individuals who have different perspectives of a situation. *Hamlet* cannot be appreciated by an audience that lacks empathy; nor, for that matter, can "Star Trek". The fact that much of television programming directed toward children may be designed so as not to require empathic skills on the part of the audience is an issue with broad ramifications, extending beyond the particular concerns of this chapter.

The affective component of empathy, as well as the cognitive component, has a major role in the response to media. The child's affective response is both a consequence of her or his understanding of the protagonist and also a factor contributing to and enhancing that understanding; that is, the viewers' feelings are cues to what is happening as well as a reaction to the situation. In addition, it is the affective component that helps sustain involvement and interest in the characters and program. A child may be stimulated and excited by a program without the mediation of empathic feeling. However, we would suggest that empathic feeling reflects a deeper engagement on the part of the viewer.

Alternatives to Empathy

As our previous remarks on empathy have indicated, there are different levels or "kinds" of empathy such that a correspondence between the affective response of the observer and the affect of the observed can stem from very different psychological processes and have very different behavioral implications. A major factor differentiating these "levels" or kinds of empathy is the degree of cognitive sophistication entailed in the empathic response. Thus, the crying response of infants to the distress cry of another infant, considered by Hoffman (1977) to constitute a rudimentary form of empathy, is largely biological and involves a minimum of cognitive mediation. Although this early affective response to affective stimuli may well contribute to more mature kinds of affective sharing that also entail perspective-taking and role-taking, from our point of view it is helpful to reserve the empathy construct for a process that integrates affective and cognitive facets.

An infant's distress reaction to another distressed infant is akin to a form of emotional contagion, like the giggling reaction to the giggling of others observed among children and the spread of panic and fear that can take place in groups of adults. The latter phenomena may involve conditioned emotional mechanisms while the infant behavior presumably reflects only wired-in biological response patterns. However, all of these emotional contagion behaviors are probably functionally different from empathic responses that involve significant cognitive components, such as affective discrimination and self–other discrimination. Thus, in contrast to the prosocial correlates that have been found for empathy as defined here, it is unlikely that emotional contagion or other forms of conditioned emotional reactions would correlate similarly with prosocial behavior.

Still other processes may produce similarity between a child's affective reaction and the affective stimuli displayed on television. For example, a young child smiling and exhibiting other happy signs while observing a happy scene in which a child actor is receiving gifts may not be responding to the emotions of the television protagonist. Rather, the child observer may be reacting "as if" the stimuli affecting the television character were directly addressed to himself or herself. Children may display fear in response to the depiction on television of some dangerous situation, not because of the fear displayed by the protagonist, but because they themselves feel directly threatened. The reactions of the protagonist may be largely irrelevant to the young child's reactions.

In the case of dramatic stimuli, it is often difficult to discriminate between an event that is experienced as directed toward a television character versus an event that is experienced as directed toward oneself. In everyday life, there are usually many cues present that facilitate sharp discriminations between the stimuli impinging on oneself and those impinging on another person. A youngster observing a peer who falls and cries may wince without any perception that (or belief that) he himself or she herself has fallen and been hurt. In this situation, the observing child probably understands and shares the feelings of the child who has fallen. To respond empathically to the feelings of another person, one may put oneself "in the other's head" as it were—perceiving situations from the other's perspective and experiencing to some degree the emotions that the other is experiencing—whether anger at being arbitrarily frustrated, pride at having achieved a difficult goal, or fear of possible failure, without losing one's separate identity. To be empathic with someone else implies the recognition of separate identities; otherwise, the affective reaction is not a shared one but an egocentric one. Empathy demands some identification coupled with maintenance of self–other boundaries.

Identification and Empathy

The role of identification in empathy is not a simple one. The mechanism or construct of identification is complex and not easily defined in operational terms. As psychoanalytic theory suggests, there are probably different types and degrees of identification. Identification, in contrast to imitation and modeling, is not a well-studied phenomenon. In media research, identification has usually been assessed through determining which character the viewer admires and wishes to be like. Imitative behavior has also been used as a criterion for identification. However, little attention has been given to the study of identification *during* the child's viewing of a television or movie drama. An analysis is required of the child's cognitions, affective reactions, and motor responses, as well as his or her subsequent reactions to the characters in the program. It may be that some degree of identification with a fantasy or real life person is required in order for empathy to occur. It may be useful to supplement the index of affective matching with other measures to determine whether the sharing of affect between a child observer and a television character reflects true empathy.

It is probably also the case that the separation of self between the child and a real person appearing on television is greater than that between the child and a fictional person. One of the differences between fantasy and reality is that reality is more constraining. Fantasy permits more possibilities—associations, modifications, transformations. Thus there is research indicating very different psychological reactions to television content that is perceived as fantasy than when the same content is perceived as depicting reality (e.g., Feshback, 1972). For this reason, it may be useful in the analysis of empathic reactions to television content, to study affective responses to news programs and documentaries as well as to television dramas.

Empirical Studies

The analysis that has been offered suggests that the empathic process does mediate certain affective responses to television. However, the analysis also suggests that "empathy like" reactions in response to television, where the viewer appears to be sharing the feelings of a television character, can result from very different mechanisms with different psychological implications. The idea that matched affect between viewer and television stimulus can have different meanings is nicely illustrated in a study by Wilson and Cantor (1984), one of the few studies that directly investigated the relationship between television and empathy.

Arguing from N. Feshbach's (1975) model of empathy, these investigators proposed that preschool children, while able to identify emotions and react to emotion eliciting stimuli, do not have the cognitive skills that would enable them to assume the role of another; that is, these children are too young to display true empathy. To demonstrate age differences in the meaning of a shared emotional reaction, they exposed 3- to 5-year-old and 9- to 10-year-old children to 2-minute variants of fear-eliciting scenes from a television movie. One variation involved a large, buzzing, and threatening bumblebee, covering most of the screen. A boy's head, with bees swarming around, was evident at the beginning of the scene. The other version displayed the frightened, sweating face of the boy, preceded by a shot of a swarm of tiny bees. The experimental segments were embedded in a series of short programs. Consistent with theoretical expectation, the older children reacted with similar levels of fear to the two sets of stimuli, while the younger children rarely reported negative feelings when viewing the frightened child but were more likely to do so when viewing the frightening stimulus. This same pattern of differences was obtained with physiological measures of emotional arousal. These findings suggest that empathy mediated the affective responses of the older children to the television stimulus but not those of the younger children.

There is evidence from studies of adults that individual differences in perspective taking and empathic concern mediate differences in affective reactions to dramatic films (Davis, Hull, Young, & Warren, 1987). Empathic individuals may report greater guilt feelings when they observe the depiction of inequity or discrimination. Empathic individuals may also prefer particular kinds of television programs. Because those higher in empathy tend to be less aggressive in their behavior, one could infer that they have less positive (or even more negative) reactions to aggression than do those lower in empathy and that these reactions would influence their television viewing behavior. A study by Davis (1983b) tested this prediction. He reported that undergraduates who display empathic concern and personal distress response to another's experience, as assessed by a questionnaire, are more likely than less empathic individuals to prefer nonaggressive drama programs such as "The Waltons." Moreover, a measure of perspective taking was inversely related to the viewing of aggressive drama, in accordance with expectation. However, the measure was also inversely related to the viewing of nonaggressive drama, rendering ambiguous the interpretation of the inverse correlation of perspective-taking with aggressive drama viewing. The emotional concern scale appears to be systematically related to television viewing behavior. In a previous study, Davis (1983a) found that an emotional concern measure was associated with more viewing and more contributions to a muscular dystrophy telethon. While emotional concern does not meet the definition of empathy that has been proposed, it is a closely related, if not derivative, disposition.

The Davis findings, as well as the writings of Hoffman (1982a), suggest that it would be useful to analyze empathy separately for positive and negative affects, particularly empathic responses to individuals experiencing sadness. In our research, we have found that while "positive" (euphoric) empathy and "negative" (dysphoric) empathy sometimes have similar correlates, there are conditions under which these measures will relate differently to cognitive and interpersonal measures. Consequently, experiencing empathy with positive or negative emotions should be distinguished when exploring the relationship of individual differences in empathy to television program viewing behaviors.

In summary, empathy has a role in mediating children's reactions to dramatic presentations on television and other media, but the role is more subtle than children's emotional reactions to media would suggest. "True" empathy involves sensitivity to the emotions and perspectives of another person and the sharing of that person's feelings without a loss of ego boundaries. Empathy is then manifested by a correspondence between the feelings of an observer and those of the individual observed. However, a correspondence between the feelings of a child viewing a television drama and the feelings of a character in that drama can come about through processes other than empathy, although dynamically related to empathy.

Effects of Television on Children's Empathy

In the previous section we considered the extent to which the empathic process may mediate reactions to media programs, particularly dramatic fare. In relation to this question, the role of individual differences in empathy in determining the response to television was briefly addressed. We now turn to another important issue of the television/empathy interaction, namely whether exposure to television influences the development of empathy and related processes in children.

Experiencing Emotions

Drama, as has been noted earlier, elicits emotional responses in the audience, the emotional properties of the dramatic experience being an essential, if not the most essential, feature of drama and of other forms of entertainment as well. Television is no exception to this rule. The emotional impact of television has been extensively reviewed by Dorr in a series of publications (Dorr, 1981, 1982; Dorr, Doubleday, & Kovaric, 1983; Huston et al., 1992) and most recently by Donnerstein and Smith in the present volume.

As these comprehensive reviews make evident, the concept of "emotional impact" embraces a variety of emotional phenomena. It is important to specify the nature of the emotional dimension or experience that is related to or influenced by television viewing. It is clear that television elicits a range of affects, including such negative emotions as fear, sadness, and disgust, and such positive emotions as pleasure and mirth (Dorr et al., 1983; Huston et al., 1992). Children, like adults, appear to enjoy the process of arousal and resolution of these feelings. They enjoy and value programmatic content that elicits affective reactions of excitement, laughter, and social warmth (Zillmann, 1980, 1982).

Recognizing Emotions

Children are attentive to cues that convey the emotions being experienced by the television characters viewed. There are important age differences in the subtlety and range of cues to which children are sensitive. Preschoolers and younger children are especially guided by the facial expression of the characters. Older children are more responsive to situational cues and are more able to understand the emotional implications that particular symbols and metaphors are intended to convey (Harris, Olthof, & Terwogt, 1981). However, younger children can be trained to better identify emotions and to better comprehend emotional situations (Feshbach & Cohen, 1988).

There are some programs such as "Mister Rogers' Neighborhood" and "Sesame Street" that have an explicit goal of teaching children to recognize and label their own and others' emotions. Although heavy viewers of "Sesame Street" have been found to be better able to associate particular emotions and relevant affective situations than light viewers, the effect was rather weak (Bogatz & Ball, 1971). The "Mister Rogers' Neighborhood" program devotes more time to affective issues than "Sesame Street," and a systematic evaluation of the effects of viewing "Mister Rogers" on children's overall empathy and its components would be of considerable interest.

From a theoretical standpoint, the portrayal of emotions can have a number of consequences for the child's psychological development. Emotional expressions are an important element in communication. As the child becomes more sensitive to emotional cues, both to their presence and absence, he or she should develop greater understanding of the possible meanings of the social situations and interactions giving rise to the emotional reactions. And, according to the previously described model of empathy (Feshbach, 1975), the recognition and discrimination of emotional cues is one of the essential components of the empathic response. In addition, the portrayal of emotions on television may provide the child with cues and models as to how emotions should be expressed. The expression of emotion in humans, unlike the case for nonhuman species, is not invariant. Emotional expression is, subject to learning and social influence.

Imagination and Prosocial Behavior

Another avenue by which television viewing might influence empathy is through enhancing the child's capacity to assume the role of others and perceive situations from other people's perspective. Here, too, there is little direct evidence that can be cited to evaluate television's actual or potential effect on this important social cognitive skill. However, there are data that bear on the influence of "Mister Rogers' Neighborhood" on children's imaginative skills (e.g., Singer & Singer, 1976; Friedrich & Stein, 1975). Because the process of empathy entails the capacity to assume another's perspective, a skill that involves an act of imagination, the impact of television programming on imagination has implications for children's empathy. Consequently, if a television program is effective in stimulating children's imagination, one can also anticipate an enhancement of empathy.

In a well-designed study, Singer and Singer (1976) experimentally varied exposure of preschool children to "Mister Rogers." They found enhancement of imaginative play skills in one of their experimental groups. However, the effect was contingent on the presence of a "mediator" who interpreted events in the program and directed children's attention to relevant program cues. No significant effects were found for the children who watched "Mister Rogers" without a mediator present. Friedrich and Stein (1975) have also reported increases in 3- to 5-year-old children's imagination following exposure to "Mister Rogers" programs. Again, other elements in the experimental treatment such as teacher training and relevant play materials may have been primarily responsible for the experimental effects.

Although not directly addressing empathy, studies on the influence of television on prosocial behavior are somewhat germane to the concerns of this chapter. In general, prosocial behaviors are believed to be mediated by or closely related to empathy. Helping individuals who are economically less fortunate is an example of a behavior that is intimately related to empathy and that has been shown to be enhanced by exposure to experimentally prepared videotapes depicting a model engaging in acts of generosity (Bryan, 1975). A similar effect has been demonstrated by children who viewed an actual television program. A group of 5-year-old children, randomly assigned to viewing a "Lassie" program in which Lassie's master risks his life to save Lassie's pup, displayed a greater willingness than comparison groups to help puppies in distress where it involved some cost to the children (Sprafkin, Liebert, & Poulos, 1975). This latter finding is of particular interest since it involves a more generalized influence than matching of a model's behavior. Generalized, prosocial effects of television were also found in an impressive experiment by Moriarty and McCabe (1977) in which children participating in various Little League sports were assigned to prosocial, antisocial, or control video presentations of the relevant team sport in which they were engaged. Although exposure to the antisocial, aggressive content did not affect player behavior, significant increases in prosocial behavior were observed in children who had been exposed to television content portraying cooperative and sympathetic behaviors, affection, reparation for wrong-doing, and concern for others.

A variety of studies have been carried out that indicate that exposure to prosocial program content can enhance socially desirable behaviors. This overall finding is clearly evident from a number of reviews of the literature (Dorr, 1986; Huston et al., 1992; Rushton, 1982). What is less evident is the stability and generality of these effects. It is possible that after prolonged exposure, the prosocial stimulus may lose its potency and viewers may become indifferent to and bored with the content. The studies carried out by Singer and Singer (1976) and Friedrich and Stein (1975) suggest that television content may have to be reinforced by other socializing influences to obtain a prosocial effect.

The extent to which the "messages" conveyed by prosocial content presented on television can generalize beyond the depicted context and behaviors is still an unresolved issue. This question is important both theoretically and pragmatically. Presumably, the greater the extent to which mediating processes associated with prosocial behaviors are influenced by television, the greater the change in prosocial behavior that can be anticipated. This is not to deny the importance of displaying specific acts of generosity, help-giving, and cooperation that children can model. But changes in mediating processes such as caring for others, role-taking, and empathy are likely to have a more powerful influence on the promulgation of prosocial behavior than changes in a specific behavior (see Ahammer & Murray, 1979). Role-playing training, in particular, may prove to be even more effective in facilitating generalization of altruistic behavior. The integration of role playing into television programming would appear to be a particularly promising approach to fostering empathy and other prosocial orientations in children.

Conclusions: Implications for Television Programming

The studies that have been reviewed indicate that a child's capacity for empathy is a critical element in a child's response to television. The reciprocal nature of the relationship between children's empathy and television provides an opportunity for television programming to capture children's interest and attention while stimulating their imagination, deepening their emotional sensitivity, and enlarging their horizons.

There are several related approaches that can be taken to modify television programming so as to further these objectives. One approach is to directly foster empathy through significant television figures engaging in role-playing and perspective-taking and manifesting empathy in their social interactions. These figures would not simply function as models for imitation, although this, in itself, would be quite desirable. More important, through their empathic reactions to the feelings of others, these dramatic characters can provide an opportunity for the child viewers to experience vicariously the processes that contribute to empathy: to be sensitive to and recognize another person's emotions, to assume another person's perspective in viewing a situation, and to experience feelings that the other person is experiencing. One can illuminate for the child the role of empathy through using dramatic devices that contrast the interactions of an empathic television character with those of a nonempathic television character. Through such devices, the child can be helped to better appreciate the possibility of alternative interpretations of the same situation and alternative ways of coping with that situation.

Television programming should also be more broadly modified to provide greater focus on the feelings, motivations, and conflicts of its dramatic characters. This can be accomplished without major content changes in current programming. For example, television programs directed toward children are typically characterized by a high degree of action. Heroes and heroines fly robot ships, attack adversaries, perform physical feats, play games, commit pranks. The feelings, ideas, motives, and perspectives of either the main or supporting players are usually given little, if any, attention. The exciting action does not have to be eliminated. However, the action could be accompanied by scenes in which the inner world of the protagonists is given attention. The feelings with which the protagonists may be struggling and the attributions they are making about themselves and others could be depicted.

We are not proposing that television action must be preceded by a deep psychological analysis of the emotional state of the individuals engaged in the action. Nevertheless, much more could be done to depict the feelings and perspectives of television characters in children's programming. Sensitivity to other people's feelings and views, and the sharing of emotional experiences, should be integrated into standard television fare. Thus, when a television character is sensitive to the feelings and viewpoint of another character, compassion, mercy, or compromise rather than aggression may be the outcome. Probably few would object to a change in this direction in the nature of television content.

Since the changes being proposed would appear relatively simple to implement, the question arises as to whether the internal life of the protagonist in action or dramatic presentations will attract a sufficiently large audience to permit the adoption of this approach by commercial television. We believe that it will. Children, as well as adults, are intrigued by and attracted to the world of feelings and desires. Children are engaged by dramatic themes of attachment, family supports and sibling conflicts, moral dilemmas, and the emotions evoked when confronting and overcoming danger.

Research is needed to evaluate the appeal of these dramatic themes to children, and to determine the effects of exposure to such television content on children's empathy and their social–emotional development. However, while awaiting the verdict of research, it would seem appropriate to proceed on the assumption that programs focusing on relationships, conflicts and their resolution, on empathy and caring, will have wide appeal for children, provided these programs are well done.

By confronting the challenge of making the medium more meaningful for children, TV executives can begin to explore and expand the richness and range of experiences that television can provide. It may be more than possible that television programming can simultaneously serve the industry and serve the best interests of the child.

REFERENCES

Ahammer, U. M., & Murray, J. P. (1979). Kindness in the kindergarten: The relative influence of role playing and prosocial television in facilitating altruism. *International Journal of Behavioral Development, 2*, 133–157.

Barnett, M. A., King, L. M., & Howard, J. A. (1979). Inducing affect about self or other: Effects on generosity in children. *Developmental Psychology, 15*, 164–167.

Bogatz, G. A., & Ball, S. (1971). *The second year of Sesame Street: A continuing evaluation*. Princeton, NJ: Educational Testing Service.

Borke, H. (1973). The development of empathy in Chinese and American children between three and six years of age. *Developmental Psychology, 9*, 102–108.

Bryan, J. H. (1975). Children's cooperation and helping behavior. In E. M. Hetherington (Ed.), *Review of child development research* (Vol. 5). Chicago: University of Chicago Press.

Collins, W. A. (1982). Cognitive processing in television viewing. In D. Peral, L. Bouthilet, & J. Lazar (Eds.), *Television and behavior: Ten years of scientific progress and implications for the eighties* (Vol. 2). Rockville, MD: National Institute of Mental Health.

Davis, M. H. (1983a). Empathic concern and the muscular dystrophy telethon: Empathy as a multidimensional construct. *Personality and Social Psychology Bulletin, 9*(2), 223–229.

Davis, M. H. (1983b). Measuring individual differences in empathy: Evidence for a multidimensional approach. *Journal of Personality and Social Psychology, 44*, 113–126.

Davis, M. H. (1983c). Measuring individual differences in empathy: Evidence of a multidimensional approach. *Journal of Personality and Social Psychology, 44*, 113–126.

Davis, M. H., Hull, J. G., Young, R. D., & Warren, G. G. (1987). Emotional reactions to dramatic film stimuli. The influence of cognitive and emotional empathy. *Journal of Personality and Social Psychology, 52*, 126–133.

Dorr, A. (1981). Television and affective development and functioning: Maybe this decade. *Journal of Broadcasting, 25*(4), 335–346.

Dorr, A. (1982). Television and affective development and functioning. In D. Pearl, L. Bouthilet, & J. Lazar (Eds.), *Television and behavior: Ten years of scientific progress and implications for the eighties* (Vol. 2). Rockville, MD: National Institute of Mental Health.

Dorr, A. (1986). *Television and children: A special medium for a special audience.* Newbury Park, CA: Sage.

Dorr, A., Doubleday, C., & Kovaric, P. (1983). Emotions depicted on and stimulated by television programs. In M. Meyer (Ed.), *Children and the formal features of television*. Munich and New York: K. G. Saur.

Eisenberg, N., & Fabes, R. A. (1990). Empathy: Conceptualization, measurement and relation to prosocial behavior. *Motivation and Emotion, 14*(2), 109–112.

Eisenberg, N., & Lennon, R. (1983). Sex differences in empathy and related capacities. *Psychological Bulletin, 94*(1), 100–131.

Eisenberg, N., & Miller, P. A. (1987). The relation of empathy to prosocial and related behaviors. *Psychological Bulletin, 101*, 91–119.

Feshbach, N. D. (1975). Empathy in children: Some theoretical and empirical considerations. *The Counseling Psychologist, 4*(2), 221–226.

Feshbach, N. D. (1978). Studies on empathic behavior in children. In B. A. Maher (Ed.), *Progress in experimental personality research* (Vol. 8). New York: Academic Press.

Feshbach, N. D. (1979). Empathy training: A field study in affective education. In S. Feshbach & A. Fraczek (Eds.), *Aggression and behavior change: Biological and social processes* (pp. 234–249). New York: Praeger.

Feshbach, N. D. (1982). Sex differences in empathy and social behavior in children. In N. Eisenberg (Ed.), *The development of prosocial behavior*. New York: Academic Press.

Feshbach, N. D. (1983). Learning to care: A positive approach to child training and discipline. *Journal of Clinical Child Psychology, 12*(3), 266–271.

Feshbach, N. D. (1984). Empathy, empathy training and the regulation of aggression in elementary school children. In R. M. Kaplan, V. J. Konecni, & R. Novoco (Eds.), *Aggression in children and youth* (pp. 192–208). The Hague, Netherlands: Martinus Nijhoff.

Feshbach, N., & Cohen, S. (1988). Training affect comprehension in young children: An experimental evaluation. *Journal of Applied Developmental Psychology, 9*, 201–210.

Feshbach, N. D., & Feshbach, S. (1982). Empathy training and the regulation of aggression: Potentialities and limitations. *Academic Psychology Bulletin, 4*, 394–413.

Feshbach, N. D., & Hoffman, M. (1978, April). Sex differences in children's reports of emotion-arousing situations. In Diane McGuiness (Chair), *Sex differences: Commotion, motion, or emotion: Psychological gender differences.* Paper presented in symposium at the meeting of the Western Psychological Association, San Francisco.

Feshbach, N. D., & Kuchenbecker, S. (1974, September). *A three-component model of empathy.* Symposium presented at the meeting of the American Psychological Association, New Orleans.

Feshbach, N. D., & Roe, K. (1968). Empathy in six and seven year olds. *Child Development, 39*, 133–145.

Feshbach, N. D., Feshbach, S., Fauvre, M., & Ballard-Campbell, M. (1983). *Learning to care: A curriculum for affective and social development.* Glenview, IL: Scott, Foresman.

Feshbach, S. (1972). Effects of reality versus fantasy in filmed violence. In J. P. Murray, E. A. Rubinstein, & G. A. Comstock (Eds.), *Television and social behavior: Television and social learning* (Vol. II). Washington, DC: US Government Printing Office.

Feshbach, S., & Feshbach, N. D. (1986). Aggression and altruism: A personality perspective. In C. Zahn-Waxler, M. Chapman, & M. Radke-Yarrow (Eds.), *Aggression and altruism: Biological and social origins.* New York: Cambridge University Press.

Friedrich, L. K., & Stein, A. H. (1975). Prosocial television and young children: The effects of verbal labeling and role playing on learning and behavior. *Child Development, 46*, 27–38.

Harris, P. L., Olthof, T., & Terwogt, M. M. (1981). Children's knowledge of emotion. *Journal of Child Psychology and Psychiatry, 22*, 247–261.

Hoffman, M. L. (1975). Developmental synthesis of affect and cognition and its implications for altruistic motivation. *Developmental Psychology, 11*, 607–622.

Hoffman, M. L. (1977). Empathy, its development and prosocial implications. In C. B. Keasey (Ed.), *Nebraska Symposium on Motivation* (Vol. 25). Lincoln: University of Nebraska Press.

Hoffman, M. L. (1982a). Development of prosocial motivation: Empathy and guilt. In N. Eisenberg (Ed.), *The development of prosocial behavior.* New York: Academic Press.

Hoffman, M. L. (1982b). Measurement of empathy. In C. Izard (Ed.), *Measuring emotions in infants and children*. New York: Cambridge University Press.

Huston, A. C., Donnerstein, E., Fairchild, H., Feshbach, N. D., Katz, P. A., Murray, J. P., Rubinstein, E. A., Wilcox, B. L., & Zuckerman, D. (1992). *Big world, small screen*. Lincoln: University of Nebraska Press.

Huston, A. C., Wright, J. C., Alvarez, M., & Truglio, R. (1995). Perceived television reality and children's emotional and cognitive responses to its social context. *Journal of Applied Developmental Psychology, 16*, 231–251.

Knowles, A. D., & Dixon, M. C. (1990). Children's comprehension of a television cartoon's emotional theme. *Australian Journal of Psychology, 42*, 115–121.

Lipps, T. (1906). Das Wissen von fremden Ichen [title translation]. *Psychologische Untersuchungen, 1*, 694–722.

McDougall, W. (1960). *An introduction to social psychology*. New York: Barnes & Noble. (Originally published 1908)

Mead, G. H. (1974). *Mind, self, and society*. Chicago: University of Chicago Press. (Originally published 1934)

Mehrabian, A., & Epstein, N. (1972). A measure of emotional empathy. *Journal of Personality, 40*(4), 525–543.

Moriarty, D., & McCabe, A. E. (1977). Studies of television and youth sport. In *Ontario. Royal Commission on Violence in the Communications Industry Report* (Vol. 5). Toronto: Queen's Printer for Ontario.

Radke-Yarrow, M., Zahn-Waxler, C., & Chapman, M. (1983). Children's prosocial dispositions and behavior. In E. M. Hetherington (Ed.), *Socialization, personality, and social development*. New York: Wiley.

Rothenberg, B. B. (1970). Child's social sensitivity and the relationship to interpersonal competence, intrapersonal comfort and intellectual level. *Developmental Psychology, 2*(3), 335–350.

Rushton, J. P. (1982). Television and prosocial behavior. In D. Pearl, L. Bouthilet, & J. Lazar (Eds.), *Television and behavior: Ten years of scientific progress and implications for the eighties* (Vol. 2). Rockville, MD: National Institute of Mental Health.

Sagi, A., & Hoffman, M. L. (1976). Empathic distress in the newborn. *Developmental Psychology, 12*, 175–176.

Simner, M. L. (1971). Newborn's response to the cry of another infant. *Developmental Psychology, 5*, 136–150.

Singer, J. L., & Singer, D. G. (1976). Fostering creativity in children: Can TV stimulate imaginative play? *Journal of Communication, 26*, 74–80.

Sprafkin, J. M., Liebert, R. M., & Poulos, R. W. (1975). Effects of a pro-social example on children's helping. *Journal of Experimental Child Psychology, 20*, 119–126.

Stotland, E., & Dunn, R. E. (1963). Empathy, self-esteem and birth order. *Journal of Abnormal and Social Psychology, 66*(6), 532–540.

Sullivan, H. S. (1953). *The interpersonal theory of psychiatry*. New York: W. W. Norton.

Wilson, B. J., & Cantor, J. (1984). *Developmental differences in empathy with a protagonist's emotion*. University of Wisconsin.

Zahn-Waxler, C., & Radke-Yarrow, M. (1982). The development of altruism: Alternative research strategies. In N. Eisenberg-Berg (Ed.), *The development of prosocial behavior*. New York: Academic Press.

Zillmann, D. (1980). Anatomy of suspense. In P. H. Tannenbaum (Ed.), *The entertainment functions of television*. Hillsdale, NJ: Erlbaum.

Zillmann, D. (1982). Television viewing and arousal. In D. Pearl, L. Bouthilet, & J. Lazar (Eds.), *Television and behavior: Ten years of scientific progress and implications for the eighties* (Vol. 2). Rockville, MD: National Institute of Mental Health.

Impact of Media Violence on Children, Adolescents, and Adults

Edward Donnerstein and Stacy L. Smith

We live in a violent society. As a nation, we rank first among all developed countries in the world in homicides. The statistics on violence are staggering, particularly in regard to children and adolescents. Consider, for example, the following figures cited by the American Psychological Association (1993):

- Among individuals 15 to 24 years old, homicide is the second leading cause of death. For African Americans in this age bracket, however, it is number one.
- Adolescents account for 24% of all violent crimes leading to arrest. The rate has increased over time for 12- to 19-year-olds and is down for individuals 35 and older.
- Every five minutes a child is arrested for a violent crime.
- Gun-related violence takes the life of an American child every 3 hours.

- Every day over 100,000 children carry guns to schools.
- In a recent survey of fifth graders in New Orleans, more than 50% of the children reported being a victim of violence, and 70% of these kids have seen weapons being used.
- A child growing up in Chicago is 15 times more likely to be murdered than a child growing up in Northern Ireland.

What accounts for these alarming figures? There is universal agreement that many factors contribute to violent behavior in society, including gangs, drugs, guns, poverty, and racism. Many of these variables may independently or interactively affect antisocial responding. Because of the complexity of these and other contributory factors, groups such as the American Psychological Association, the American Medical Association, the National Academy of Science, and the Centers for Disease Control and Prevention have examined extensively the multiple causes of violence. Cutting across all these investigations was a profound realization that the mass media also contributes to aggressive behavior in our country.

We realize that there is no single cause to violent behavior. We also realize that media violence is not the most important contributor to antisocial actions. Furthermore, it is not every violent act on television or in film that is of concern. Nor is it every child or adult who will act aggressively after watching a violent media portrayal. But there is clear evidence, as we will see in this chapter, that exposure to media violence can contribute to aggressive behavior in viewers. This conclusion is based on careful and critical readings of over 40 years of social scientific research. Before examining this literature, however, it is important to examine what types of violent images are portrayed in the mass media, particularly on television.

What Types of Violent Images Appear in the Mass Media?

Americans watch an enormous amount of TV. Recent surveys have indicated that nearly 98% of American households have a television and many have more than one set (Huston et al., 1992; Children Now, 1995). Within these homes, 2- to 11-year-olds have the TV set turned on for approximately 28 hours a week and 13- to 19-year-olds for roughly 23 hours a week. These patterns have been found consistently over many years of research.

It is now widely known that television viewing occupies more time than any other nonschool activity. And among children, it accounts for more than half of all their leisure activities. Furthermore, Black and Hispanic children have been found to view more television independent of their level of social economic status (Tangey & Feshbach, 1988). Many of the poorest and potentially most vulnerable groups in society are the heaviest viewers of television (i.e., Kuby & Csikszentmihalyi, 1990).

If children watch an average 2 to 4 hours of television per day (Huston et al., 1992), how much violence are they being exposed to? Research indicates that by the time a child leaves elementary school, he or she will have seen approximately 8,000 murders and more than 100,000 other acts of violence (Huston et al., 1992). Near the end of their teenage years, they will have witnessed over 200,000 violent acts on television (Huston et al., 1992). These figures will be significantly higher if the child has access to premium cable programming or violent films he or she can rent and watch on a VCR.

Numerous content analyses have assessed the amount and types of violent portrayals that are featured on television programming. For example, one study indicated that there are approximately 5 to 6 violent acts per hour on prime-time television and 20 to 25 violent acts per hour on Saturday morning children's fare (Gerbner & Signorielli, 1990). Within the United States, this accounts for approximately 188 hours of violent programming per week, or about 15% of program time (Huesmann, 1992). In addition to broadcast television, cable TV adds to the level of violence by airing new, more violent programs, and by recycling older violent broadcasts.

One survey by the Center for Media and Public Affairs (Lichter & Amundson, 1992) identified 1,846 violent scenes on broadcast and cable television between 6:00 a.m. and midnight across one day of programming that aired in Washington, DC. The most violent periods were between 6:00 a.m. and 9:00 a.m. (i.e., 497 violent scenes identified) and between 2:00 p.m. and 5:00 p.m. (i.e., 609 violent scenes identified). Clearly, most of the violence was aired when children were most likely to be in the viewing audience. In addition to frequency, this study also assessed the different types of violence that were portrayed. Serious assaults accounted for 20% of the violence, and 18% was accounted for by gunplay.

Now that television content has expanded to include R-rated movies, another related concern surrounds the types of characters that are being victimized by violence. A content analysis has revealed that in popular R-rated "horror" films, women are killed at a ratio of almost 3 to 1 compared with prime-time television, and 2 to 1 compared to other R-rated films (Linz & Donnerstein, 1994). In addition, there is an association in these films of sexual content with the victimization of females. The analyses showed that 33% of occurrences of sex were connected to violence (male or female). Fourteen percent of all sex incidents were linked to the death of a woman. Furthermore, nearly 22% of all innocent female protagonists were killed during or following a sexual display or act. These findings are important to note given the presence of cable TV, which has allowed even young children to view R-rated films on television.

Perhaps surprisingly, the level of violence on *broadcast* television has remained relatively constant over the last two decades (Gerbner, 1992). The rates for cable television, however, have not yet been systematically studied. Recently, the National Cable Television Association (NCTA) agreed to monitor violence on both cable and broadcast networks for three consecutive years. The first yearly report, of the 1994–1995 viewing session, was recently released by the National Television Violence Study (1996). This study examined cable and broadcast television in a manner different from all other content analyses of television violence. The investigation had two primary goals: (a) to identify the contextual features associated with violent depictions that most significantly increase the risk of a harmful effect on the audience, and (b) to analyze the television environment in depth in order to report on the nature and extent of violent depictions, focusing in particular on the relative presence of the most problematic portrayals.

In this study, violence was defined as an overt depiction of physical force, or the credible threat of such force, intended to physically harm an animate being or group of beings. Violence also included certain depictions of physically harmful consequences against an animate being or group of beings that occur as a result of unseen violent means. The study analyzed content at three distinct levels. At each level, specific contextual measures were assessed.

The first and most micro level is the violent interaction. A violent interaction is an aggressive exchange that takes place between a perpetrator and a target involving a particular type of act. For each interaction, the following contextual variables were assessed: demographic and attributive qualities of perpetrators and targets, type of violent act, the reason for the act, means used in the act, extent of means used, harm or pain that occurred from the act, likely harm that would result from the act in real life, and the presence of sexual assault. The second level is the violent scene. A violent scene is a sequence of interrelated or con-tiguous violent interactions. After each scene,[1] the following contextual features were ascertained: rewards, punishments, humor, graphicness, and explicitness. The third and most macro level is the overall violent program. A program is considered violent if anything in its unfolding narrative met the aforementioned definition of violence. At the program level, the following contextual factors were assessed: message about violence, long-term harm or pain, pattern of punishments, and realism.

The researchers (i.e., Wilson et al., 1996) randomly selected programs from 23 broadcast and cable television channels over a 20-week period of time ranging from October of 1994 to June of 1995. Thus, a compos-ite week of television content was compiled for each programming source. Programs were selected between the hours of 6:00 a.m. and 11:00 p.m. across all seven days of the week, yielding a sum of approx-imately 119 hours per channel. In total then, this project examined approximately 2,500 hours of television programming, or 2,693 pro-grams. This is the largest and most representative sample of television content ever assembled and assessed in the history of social science research.

The results from this study indicated that a majority of the pro-grams analyzed contained violence (57%).[2] Premium cable was more likely to contain violence, whereas the broadcast networks and par-ticularly public broadcasting were less likely. The majority of perpe-trators and targets of violence were adult, White, and male. In 25% of all violent interactions, guns were used. Violence was rarely punished in the immediate or following scene. When it was punished, however, it was usually directed towards "bad" characters at the end of the pro-

---

[1] All scene-level contextual variables were assessed after coders watched the scene and the immediate scene that followed. The rationale for having coders watch the following scene was based on the fact that rewards and pun-ishments may not be delivered or given to perpetrators until the imminent threat of violence is over. As such, coders were always instructed to watch the next scene prior to making their scene-level contextual judgments.

[2] Per contract with NCTA, The National Television Violence Study only analyzed "entertainment" and "reality-based" programming for violence. As such, breaking news, sporting events, game shows, infomercials, religious programming, and instructional shows were not assessed or coded for violence.

gram. In terms of the consequences of violence, it was found that (a) roughly half (e.g., approximately 9,000) of all violent interactions on television (e.g., approximately 18,000) feature no observable harm or pain to the victim; (b) children's series contain the highest percentage of interactions involving unrealistic levels of harm; and (c) only 16% of all violent programs depict the long-term negative consequences of violence.

As this section of the chapter has illustrated, a majority of television programs in the United States are filled with images of violence and aggression. This has been documented across several different content analyses of both broadcast and cable programming. Studies have also shown that violence and sex are often presented concurrently in horror or "slasher" films featured on cable programming. One cannot help but inquire, "What types of effects do such portrayals have on children, adolescents, and adults?" The answer to this question will be the focus of the next section.

What Does the Research Community Conclude?

Over the last few decades, many governmental and professional organizations have conducted exhaustive reviews of social scientific research on the relationship between media violence and aggressive behavior. These investigations have consistently acknowledged that media violence, across various genres, may be related to aggressive behavior in many children, adolescents, and adults, and may influence their perceptions and attitudes about real-world violence.

Two early, major reports from the U.S. government, the 1972, Surgeon General's Scientific Advisory Committee on Television and Social Behavior's (SACTSB) report and the 10-year follow-up from the National Institute of Mental Health (NIMH, 1982), concluded that television occupied a significant role in the lives of both children and adults. Both of these reports were unanimous in their claim that many types of televised violence can influence aggressive behavior. The surgeon general's report concluded that there was a significant and consistent correlation between viewing television violence and aggressive behavior. This finding emerged across many different measures of aggressive behavior and across different methodological approaches (e.g., correlational investigations, experimental studies, longitudinal field studies) to studying the problem. The surgeon general's research made clear that there was a direct, causal link between exposure to television violence and subsequent aggressive behavior by the viewer (Surgeon General's SACTSB, 1972).

The NIMH (1982) report added to the conclusions of the surgeon general's report in two significant ways. First, the age range of the effects could be extended to include preschoolers and older adolescents, and were generalizable to both genders. Research had shown that both boys and girls were affected by exposure to televised violence. Second, and perhaps more important, it was established that viewers may learn more than aggressive behavior from watching television violence. They may also learn to fear becoming a victim of violence. Heavy viewing may lead to aggression, but for some individuals it will lead to fear and apprehension about being aggressed against in the real world. It is more than aggressive behavior, the report concluded, that should be of concern.

In recent years additional reports, particularly from the Centers for Disease Control and Prevention (1991), the National Academy of Science (NAS, 1993), the American Psychological Association (1993), and Eron, Gentry, and Schlegel (1994), have lent further support to the contribution of the mass media to aggressive attitudes and behavior. The most comprehensive of these reports came from the American Psychological Association, which established a Commission on Youth and Violence in 1992 to exhaustively examine the scientific literature on the causes and prevention of violence. Like previous investigations into violence, the role of the mass media was considered and the conclusions reached were similar. Specifically, the APA's report concluded that nearly four decades of research on television viewing and other media have documented the almost universal exposure of American children to high levels of media violence, and that there is absolutely no doubt that those who are heavy viewers of this violence demonstrate increased acceptance of aggressive attitudes and increased aggressive behavior (Donnerstein, Slaby, & Eron, 1994).

Furthermore, this correlation between viewing violence on television and exhibiting aggressive behavior is fairly stable over time, place, and demographics (Huesmann & Eron, 1986), and also across varieties of television genres (Paik & Comstock, 1994). An examination of hundreds of experimental and longitudinal studies supported the position that viewing violence in the mass media is related to aggressive behavior (Huston et al., 1992). More important, naturalistic field studies and cross-national studies supported the position that the viewing of televised aggression leads to increases in subsequent aggression and that such behavior can become part of a lasting behavioral pattern (e.g., Huesmann & Eron, 1986). Aggressive habits learned early in life form the foundation for later behavior. Aggressive children who have trouble in school and difficulty relating to peers tend to watch more television; the violence they see there, in turn, reinforces their tendency toward aggression. These effects are both short-term and long-term. In fact, Huesmann and his colleagues (i.e., Huesmann, 1986; Huesmann, Eron, Lefkowitz, & Walder, 1984) found a clear and significant relationship between early exposure to televised violence at age 8 and adult aggressive behavior (e.g., seriousness of criminal acts) 22 years later. As Huesmann noted,

> Aggressive habits seem to be learned early in life, and once established, are resistant to change and predictive of serious adult antisocial behavior. If a child's observation of media violence promotes the learning of aggressive habits, it can have harmful lifelong consequences. Consistent with this theory, early television habits are in fact correlated with adult criminality. (Huesmann, 1986, pp. 129–130)

Consequently, children's exposure to violence in the mass media, particularly at young ages, can have lifelong consequences.

In addition to increasing violent behaviors toward others, viewing violence on television changes attitudes and behaviors toward violence in two significant ways. First, prolonged viewing of media violence can lead to emotional desensitization toward real-world violence and the victims of violence, which can result in callous attitudes toward aggression directed at others and a decreased likelihood to take action on behalf of the victim when violence occurs (e.g., Donnerstein, Slaby, & Eron, 1994). Research on desensitization to media violence has shown that although observers react initially with relatively intense physiological responses to scenes of violence, habituation can occur with prolonged or repeated exposure to these scenes, and this habituation can carry over to other settings (e.g., Thomas, Horton, Lippencott, & Drabman, 1977). Once viewers are emotionally "comfortable" with violent content, they may also evaluate media violence more favorably in other domains (e.g., Linz, Donnerstein, & Penrod, 1988).

Second, viewing violence can increase fear of becoming a victim of violence, with a resultant increase in self-protective behaviors and increased mistrust of others. Research by Gerbner and his colleagues (i.e., Gerbner, Gross, Signorielli, & Morgan, 1986) has shown that heavy viewers of media violence tend to have a perception of social reality that "matches" that which is presented in the mass media. Heavy viewers tend to see the world as more crime-ridden and dangerous, and are more fearful of walking alone in their own neighborhoods. Furthermore, viewing violence increases viewers' appetites for becoming involved in violence or exposing themselves to violence (APA, 1993).

In summary, the research literature over the last three decades as examined by the APA and other groups has been highly consistent in recognizing that there are three major effects that occur as a result of exposure to media violence. First, there is increased violence toward others due primarily to the effect of *learning and imitation*. Second, there is increased callousness toward violence among others, which has commonly been labeled the *desensitization* effect. And third, there is increased apprehension about becoming a victim of violence, often referred to as the *fear* effect. In the following section, we will overview the major theoretical explanations for each of these effects.

What Theoretical Models Account for the Three Effects of Exposure to Media Violence?

Imitation and Learning

As we noted earlier, there is general consensus that viewers learn both aggressive behaviors and attitudes from exposure to media violence. Theoretically, one might ask, "What accounts for these effects?" One explanation is social learning theory (Bandura, 1971). This theory holds that modes of response are acquired either through direct experience or through indirect observation of models, like those presented in the mass media. Through the observation of mass media models, the viewer comes to learn which behaviors are "appropriate" or will later be rewarded from those that are "inappropriate" or will later be punished. Implicit in this approach is the assumption that most human behavior is voluntarily directed toward attaining some anticipated reward.

Many laboratory studies have demonstrated that children and adults acquire novel behaviors through observing models (e.g., Bandura, 1965; Bandura, Ross, & Ross, 1961, 1963a, 1963b; Berkowitz & Geen, 1967;

Liebert & Baron, 1972). Typically, these studies have involved exposing children or adults to an aggressive model who is either rewarded or punished for his or her behavior. After watching a model who is positively reinforced for aggression, the observers are more likely to behave in a similar manner. These studies suggested that viewing a model's aggressive behavior could inhibit or disinhibit aggressive responding. It was assumed that a model's actions could come to serve as informative cues that signal probable consequences for observers, prompting them to behave in similar ways if rewarded, inhibiting them if punished.

Research outside the laboratory has also been supportive of the social learning model (i.e., Comstock & Paik, 1991). For example, Huesmann and Eron (1986) suggested that aggression, as a characteristic way of solving problems, is learned at a young age and becomes more impervious to change as the child grows older. In a longitudinal study designed to examine the long-term effects of television violence on aggressive and criminal behavior, Huesmann, Eron, Lefkowitz, and Walder (1984) studied a group of youths in Columbia County, New York, over a 22-year period of time. This study collected data on aggression and television viewing when subjects were 8, 18, and 30 years old.

The researchers found evidence of a 22-year longitudinal effect. For boys, early viewing of television violence at age 8 correlated with self-reported aggression at age 30 (especially aggression under the influence of alcohol) and added a significant increment to the prediction of seriousness of criminal arrests accumulated by age 30 (as recorded by New York State). These effects occurred independently of social class, intellectual functioning, and parenting variables (Huesmann, 1986). Huesmann and Eron (1986) have concluded that early exposure to television violence stimulates aggression over several years, and that early aggression is a statistical precursor of later criminal behavior, leading to the longitudinal relation from habitual childhood exposure to television violence to adult crime. Their analyses suggested that approximately 10% of the variability in later criminal behavior can be attributed to television violence.

This relatively straightforward "learning" approach has gained wide acceptance among media scholars. Most research in the ensuing years has centered on those variables that facilitate the acquisition of aggressive responses through observational learning. In a latter section of this chapter, we will review those "contextual" variables that mediate the influence of aggressive models.

In the last decade, however, researchers have taken issue with the idea that neither classical conditioning perspectives nor other traditional learning theories give a full account of the effects of exposure to violent mass media (Berkowitz, 1984). Berkowitz and his colleagues (Berkowitz & Rogers, 1986) have proposed that far from being firmly learned patterns of response, many media effects are immediate, transitory, and relatively short-lived. As such, Berkowitz and others have offered an explanation influenced by theorizing in cognitive psychology (Neisser, 1967). Basically, the explanation is as follows: When people witness an event through the mass media, ideas are activated that for a short period of time tend to "prime" or evoke other semantically related thoughts. After an idea is activated, there is a greater likelihood that it and associated thought elements will come to mind again. This process of thought activation has been termed a "priming effect." Berkowitz suggested, for instance, that aggressive ideas brought on by viewing violence in the mass media can prime other semantically related thoughts, increasing the probability that they will come to mind. Once these additional thoughts come to mind, they influence aggressive responding in a variety of ways.

Berkowitz's explanation is appealing because it provides a way of unifying several tangents of mass media research by invoking one relatively simple explanation. For example, one of the contextual variables we will examine later is the viewer's identification with attractive media characters. This theoretical model suggests that viewers who identify with certain actors may imagine themselves as these characters and may envision themselves carrying out the celebrities' depicted actions. Identification with characters in the mass media should activate high imagery thoughts, and the subsequent priming of these ideas might influence subsequent behavior. It is as if viewers draw a lesson from what they see: "What happens on the screen might also happen to me if I engage in the same behavior."

Many studies provide direct and indirect evidence for the notion that the activation of aggressive ideas through exposure to violence in the mass media primes other aggression-related thoughts, which in turn may have important social consequences. In a study by Carver, Ganellen, Froming, and Chambers (1983), participants who were presented with a brief film depicting a hostile interaction between a businessman and his secretary evaluated an ambiguous stimulus person as more hostile. In another experiment (Berkowitz, Parker, & West; cited in Berkowitz, 1973, pp. 125–126), children who read aggressive comic books were more likely to choose words with aggressive connotations to complete sentences later presented by the experimenters than participants who had read neutral comic books. Other studies have shown that people who have witnessed certain types of violent encounters through the mass media (e.g., depictions of sexual violence) are more likely to favor violence in interpersonal situations (Malamuth & Check, 1981).

There is also evidence to suggest that being primed with aggressive thoughts often leads to aggressive acts. Carver et al. (1983) found that men who were induced to have aggressive thoughts by means of a sentence completion task delivered the most intense electric shocks to other men. Other studies have obtained similar findings (e.g., Worchel, 1972).

In summary, media depictions of violence, from either a modeling approach or a cognitive perspective, have a high likelihood of being emulated. One issue that can be taken with the above theorizing, however, is that it is primarily one-sided. Media effects are presumed to arise from the environment. There is no attempt to account for the recipient's expectations, active audience processing of messages, or the continued interaction of the viewer with the mass media. This one-sided approach has left a very important question unaddressed. That is, "What are the consequences of exposure to mass media violence for future violent media use?" Once the individual has been exposed to mass media violence is he or she altered in a way so that future goals and plans incorporate violence viewing? We can attempt to answer this question by describing a recent theoretical model that emphasizes the reciprocal nature of the viewer and the media event. That model is Huesmann's (1986) developmental theory of mass media violence effects.

Huesmann draws on ideas in social cognitive theory to explain the effects of televised violence, especially the notion that learning the appropriate course of action in a situation involves the retention of behavioral rules or "scripts" through mental rehearsal. In this model, as in social cognitive theory, social strategies learned through watching violent television content are tried in the immediate environment. If these strategies are reinforced, they are retained and used again. The most important contribution of the social developmental model is the explication of how personal and *interpersonal* factors intervene and link violence viewing and aggression.

Past empirical research has established five variables that are particularly important in maintaining the television viewing–aggression relation (see Huesmann, 1986). These five variables include a child's (a) intellectual achievement, (b) social popularity, (c) identification with the television characters, (d) belief in the realism of violence, and (e) level of fantasizing about aggression. According to Huesmann, a heavy diet of television violence sets into motion a sequence of processes, based on these personal and interpersonal factors, that results not only in the viewers' being more aggressive but also in their developing increased interest in seeing more television violence.

Research suggests that children who have poorer academic skills behave more aggressively. They also watch television with greater regularity, watch more violent television programs, and believe violent programs are accurate portrayals of life (Huesmann & Eron, 1986). Huesmann (1986) speculated that aggressiveness interferes with social interactions between the viewer and his or her teachers and peers that are needed to develop academic potential. Slow intellectual achievement may be related to heightened viewing of television violence for two specific reasons. First, heightened television viewing in general may interfere with intellectual achievement (Lefkowitz, Eron, Walder, & Huesmann, 1977). It may also be that children who cannot obtain gratification from success in school turn to television programming to obtain vicariously the successes they cannot otherwise obtain.

Aggressive children may also be substantially less popular with their peers (Huesmann & Eron, 1986). Longitudinal analyses suggest, however, that the relationship between unpopularity and aggression is bidirectional. Not only do more aggressive children become less popular, but less popular children seem to become more aggressive. In addition, less popular children view more television and therefore see more violence on television.

Identification with television characters may also be an important factor. Children who perceive themselves similar to television characters are more likely to be influenced by the aggressive scripts they observe (Huesmann, Lagerspetz, & Eron, 1984). This may be particularly true for boys. At the same time more aggressive children tend to identify with aggressive characters, and those who identify more with aggressive television characters behave more aggressively.

For an aggressive behavioral script to be encoded in memory and maintained, it must be salient to a child. Huesmann speculated that realistic portrayals are relatively salient depictions. If a violent action is perceived as completely unrealistic, it is unlikely that it will receive very much attention. Early investigations of televised violence have found that realistic portrayals are an important predictor of imitative effects (e.g., Feshbach, 1972). Later investigations by Huesmann and his colleagues have confirmed that the relation between violence viewing and aggression is heightened for children who believe the violence is representative of real life (Huesmann et al., 1984).

Finally, the maintenance of aggressive scripts might be accomplished through the rehearsal of these scripts in the child's mind. Research has shown that children's self-reports of violent fantasies are positively correlated with both aggression and greater television viewing (Huesmann & Eron, 1986).

Desensitization

In addition to learning aggressive attitudes and behaviors, the impact of media violence on the viewer's emotions is also of concern. Over the years, research on affective reactions to violent messages has been concerned with the possibility that continued exposure to violence in the mass media will undermine feelings of concern, empathy, or sympathy viewers might have toward victims of actual violence. The early research on desensitization to media violence has involved exposure to rather mild forms of television violence for relatively short periods of time (e.g., Cline, Croft, & Courrier, 1973; Thomas, 1982; Thomas, Horton, Lippincott, & Drabman, 1977). These studies indicated that (a) heavy viewers of media violence showed less physiological reactivity to violent film clips compared with light viewers, (b) general physiological arousal decreases as viewers continually watch violent media, and (c) children exposed to media violence are slower to respond to depictions of real aggression.

Research on longer-term exposure and more graphic forms of violence have shown similar desensitization effects. For example, Linz, Donnerstein, and Penrod (1984, 1987) measured the reactions of college-aged men to films portraying violence against women, often in a sexual context, viewed across a 5-day period. Comparisons of first and last day reactions to the films showed that, with repeated exposure, initial levels of self-reported anxiety decreased substantially. Furthermore, participants' perceptions of the films also changed from the first day to the last day. Material that was previously judged to be violent and degrading to women was seen as significantly less so by the end of the exposure period. Participants also indicated they were less depressed and enjoyed the material more with repeated exposure. Most important, these effects generalized to a victim of sexual assault presented in a videotaped reenactment of a rape trial. Participants who were exposed to the sexually violent films rated the victim as less severely injured compared with a no-exposure control group.

In another study (Linz, Donnerstein, & Penrod, 1988), participants were also less sympathetic to the rape victim portrayed in the trial and less able to empathize with rape victims in general, compared with a no-exposure control group and participants exposed to other types of films. Longer film exposure was necessary to affect the violence-viewing participants' general empathetic response.

Theoretically, Linz et al. (1984, 1988) suggested that the viewers were becoming comfortable with anxiety-provoking situations. Furthermore, it was suggested that self-awareness of reductions in anxiety and emotional arousal may be instrumental in the formation of other perceptions and attitudes about the violence portrayed in the films that are then carried over to other contexts. This position is similar to that offered in the behavioral treatment of pathological fears from exposure therapy. This research demonstrates that simply exposing a patient to the situations or objects he or she is afraid of will significantly diminish the anxiety or negative affect that was once evoked by the objects or situations (Foa & Kozak, 1986).

Similar processes may operate when subjects are repeatedly exposed to graphic media violence. Once viewers are emotionally "comfortable" with the violent content of the films, they may also evaluate the film more favorably in other domains. Material originally believed to be offensive or degrading to the victims of violence may be evaluated as less so with continued exposure. A reduction in the level of anxiety may also blunt viewers' awareness of the frequency and intensity of violence in the films. Reductions in anxiety may serve to decrease sensitivity to emotional cues associated with each violent episode and thereby reduce viewers' perceptions of the amount of violence in the films. Consequently, by the end of an extensive exposure period, viewers may perceive aggressive films as less violent than they had initially. These altered perceptual and affective reactions may then be carried over into judgments made about victims of violence in other more realistic settings.

Fear

As we noted earlier, the viewing of media violence can lead to fright reactions that can be quite stable over time (i.e, general fear of crime or being a victim), or rather transitory and fleeting in nature (i.e., immediate emotional fright reaction in a child). These effects occur in both children and adults. One theoretical explication of individuals' long-term reactions to media violence is cultivation theory. Initially developed by George Gerbner and his colleagues (i.e., Gerbner, 1969; Gerbner & Gross, 1976; Gerbner, Gross, Morgan, & Signorielli, 1994), cultivation theory presumes that extensive, cumulative exposure to the mass media shapes individuals' perceptions of social reality.

The assumption is that social actors learn facts about the "real" world from observing the world of television. Researchers have suggested that we store these facts automatically (Shapiro, 1991) and subsequently utilize this information to formulate our perceptions and beliefs about the world (e.g., Harris, 1994). As Tan (1986) noted, one of the most important mass media effects might be on the individual's conception of social reality. The media are able to determine what and when we think about our social world. They communicates the facts, norms, and values of our society through selective presentations of social events. For many individuals, television is the main source of information about critical aspects of their social environments. Learning about violence in the news and in fictional programming may lead to the belief that the world is generally a scary and dangerous place.

As research has indicated, heavy viewers believe the world they live in is more violent and unsafe, when compared with light viewers. This is suggested by heavy viewers' (a) fear of walking alone at night, (b) use of guns, locks, and dogs for protection, (c) mistrust of police, (d) estimations of the prevalence of violence, and (e) overall fear of crime (e.g., Gerbner & Gross, 1976). These results seem to indicate that the mass media contribute to the cultivation of fear. These effects have occurred with both children and adult viewers.

Cultivation theory has been criticized on both methodological (Rubin, Perse, & Taylor, 1988) and conceptual (Potter, 1993) grounds. There is a general belief that the theory is too simplistic and that a number of mediating factors influence this process (see Wilson, 1995). For example, factors such as experience with crime, motivations for viewing television, and overall cognitive abilities seem to be important components in determining the cultivation effect. Comstock and Paik (1991) have noted that the fear effect might not be cumulative at all. Instead, these scholars argued that

> exposure to violent television stimuli may simply activate or heighten
> the likelihood of recall of thoughts of a more pessimistic nature.
> Frequency of exposure in this instance may not be a measure of the

history of viewing but the likelihood of recent exposure to violence or distressing events in entertainment, news, or other programming. (Comstock & Paik, 1991, pp. 185–186)

In addition, Gunter (1994) has noted that the effect may be program specific, rather than an effect of total TV viewing. Content-specific programs, such as crime-related shows, would be most influential in affecting perceptions of crime. Or, the effects may be due to how the viewer perceives and interprets the content, particularly if they see the program as being more realistic (Potter, 1986). And finally, individuals may selectively attend to those programs that reinforce their perception of the world (Gunter, 1994).

In a recent overview of their theory, Gerbner and his colleagues acknowledged these criticisms and noted the following:

> The elements of cultivation do not originate with television or appear out of a void. Layers of social, personal, and cultural contexts also determine the shape, scope, and degree of the contribution television is likely to make. Yet, the meaning of those contexts and factors are in themselves aspects of the cultivation process. That is, although a viewer's gender, or age, or class makes a difference in perspective, television viewing can make a similar and interacting difference. . . . The interaction is a continuous process (as is cultivation) beginning with infancy and going on from cradle to grave. (Gerbner, Gross, Morgan, & Signorielli, 1994, p. 23)

For cultivation theory, viewing television is a lifelong process. Whether television shapes or maintains beliefs about the world is not as important as its role in a dynamic process that leads to enduring and stable assumptions about the world, particularly violence.

For children, however, the effect may not be so general. That is, younger viewers may not believe that the world is a mean and scary place. Children's reactions may be more specific, immediate, and urgent. Fright reactions to violent forms of media can be instantaneous and dramatic. For example, a child may scream or hide his or her eyes from a frightening depiction. Later, nightmares and recurring thoughts may keep both children and their parents awake at night (Wilson & Cantor, 1985).

There is a growing body of research that suggests that both younger and older children can experience strong emotional reactions, such as fear and anxiety, from viewing media depictions of criminal activities, violence, physical injury, or danger (see Wilson, 1995; Cantor, 1994;

Cantor & Wilson, 1988). However, research also indicates that children at different levels of cognitive development are frightened by different types of portrayals (see Cantor, 1994). Younger children, for example, respond with more fear to those fantastic depictions of threat that look scary or frightening (Cantor & Sparks, 1984; Sparks, 1986). Older children, on the other hand, respond with more fear to realistic and abstract portrayals of danger that could possibly occur in the real world (Cantor & Sparks, 1984; Sparks, 1986).

Although most of this research on children's emotional reactions has assessed immediate or short-term impact, there is research to suggest that the effects of viewing scary or frightening media can last several days or weeks (see Cantor, 1994). Some of these longer-lasting effects may be relatively mild, whereas others may be acute and disabling. That is, a child may experience a severe anxiety state after viewing violence that may last up to several weeks (Mathai, 1983). As Cantor has noted, transitory fright reactions occur in a large proportion of children, with more enduring reactions affecting an "appreciable" minority of viewers.

To account for these fear reactions, it has been suggested that a process similar to stimulus generalization might be operating. Although the viewer is in no "real" danger from viewing a violent media depiction, portrayals that would lead to danger in the real world are capable of producing fear reactions, although of a less intense nature. Cantor and her colleagues (Cantor, 1994; Cantor & Wilson, 1988; Wilson & Cantor, 1985) have suggested that three types of stimuli readily produce these reactions: (a) danger and injuries, (b) distortions of human characters, and (c) situations in which others are in fear or danger. Each of these are quite common elements in violent programming.

Furthermore, there are three important factors that mediate a fear effect. First, the more similar the depiction to real life, the stronger the reaction. Depictions of real-life events would, according to Cantor (1994), be more influential than cartoons. A second factor is the motivations of the viewer for selecting particular media depictions. In particular, older children may select or seek out frightening media fare because of its arousal or entertaining properties. For many of these viewers, the emotional impact may be heightened as they attempt to minimize the mediated aspect of the depiction (i.e., Zillmann, 1982; Cantor, 1994). Likewise, viewers who self-select certain media to become more familiar with an issue (e.g., the Oklahoma City Bombing) might be more emotionally affected because they "pay particular attention to whether or not the events portrayed are real or fictional" (Cantor, 1994, p. 227). Finally, factors that generally contribute to emotional reactions, like physiological arousal, will also increase fright reactions.

In sum, we have reviewed those theoretical perspectives that account for how media violence contributes to learning of aggressive thoughts or behaviors, desensitization, and fear in viewers. Several perspectives were advanced and each suggested that different types of violent portrayals may increase the risk of different effects on viewers. One cannot help but inquire, "Do all violent portrayals pose the same risk to viewers?" Social science research indicates that they do not. In the next section, therefore, we will delineate eight "contextual" features of violence that have been found by social scientific research to either increase or decrease the risk of the three aforementioned harmful effects.

What Contextual Features of Violent Portrayals in the Media Contribute to a Harmful Effect?

As noted above, the research community has concluded that exposure to media violence may contribute to aggression, fear, and desensitization in viewers (American Psychological Association, 1993; Centers for Disease Control, 1991). Social science research also indicates, however, that not all violent portrayals pose the same risk to viewers (Wilson et al., 1996). For example, the violence in an action-adventure film like *The Terminator* may facilitate aggressive thoughts and behaviors in viewers, whereas the violence in a dramatic movie such as *Boyz in the Hood* may actually inhibit such responding.

Clearly, this example illuminates that the context within which violence is presented affects viewers' reactions. What specific contextual factors increase or decrease the risk of harmful effects in viewers? Researchers have assessed nine different contextual cues and their influence on individuals' aggressive responding, fear, or emotional desensitization to media violence. Those nine features include the following: (a) attractiveness of the perpetrator, (b) attractiveness of the target, (c) the justification of violence, (d) the presence of weapons, (e) the extent and graphicness of violence, (f) the degree of realism of violence, (g) whether violence is rewarded or punished, (h) the consequences of violence, and (i) whether humor accompanies violence. Each contextual feature and its impact on viewers will be briefly described below. For a fuller and more detailed explication of each factor and its effects on both children and adults, see the scientific papers of the National Television Violence Study (1996).[3]

The first contextual feature is the attractiveness of the perpetrator. Violent perpetrators come in all shapes and sizes. For instance, a perpetrator may be a cultural hero such as Arnold Schwarzenegger, an anthropomorphized animal like Bugs Bunny, or a supernatural creature such as "The Blob." In addition to these different types, perpetrators may also have different motives or attributive qualities. Some may be good and act violently to protect the society, whereas others may be bad and use violence as a means to a selfish end. These examples illuminate some of the different types and motives of characters who perpetrate violence on television.

What types of perpetrators increase the risk of a harmful effect on viewers? Researchers have found that the aggressive actions of attractive perpetrators are more likely to be imitated than are those aggressive actions of unattractive perpetrators (Leyens & Picus, 1973; Liss, Reinhardt, & Fredriksen, 1983; Perry & Perry, 1976). One reason for this is that children and adults attend to, and learn from, attractive role models significantly more than they do from unattractive ones (Bandura, 1986, 1994). Social science research indicates that three specific qualities increase the attractiveness of violent perpetrators. Those three qualities are prosocial orientation, hero status, and demographic similarity between the perpetrator and viewer (Jose & Brewer, 1984; Turner & Berkowitz, 1972; Zillmann & Cantor, 1977).

The second contextual feature is the attractiveness of the target or victim of violence. Targets of violence, just like perpetrators, vary greatly in terms of their demographics, motives, and attributive qualities. Similar to the attractiveness of the perpetrator, attractiveness of the target is an important contextual cue that affects viewers' responses to aggressive portrayals. Attractive targets of violence, however, elicit a different reaction in viewers than do attractive perpetrators. When attractive characters fall prey to violence, it may evoke fear or anxiety in audience members (Wilson et al., 1996, p. 18). In explication, studies have found that audience members often experience the same feelings and affective states that attractive characters experience (Comisky & Bryant, 1982;

---

[3] In the scientific papers of the National Television Violence Study, each study assessing the effects of a particular contextual feature is reviewed in depth.

Feshbach & Roe, 1968; Zillmann, 1980, 1991; Zillmann & Cantor, 1977). Wilson and her colleagues have argued that when attractive characters become victimized by violence, viewers may empathetically share their anxiety and experience some level of fear or distress (1996, p. 19).

The third contextual feature is the justification of violence. Violence may be used for a variety of reasons in television programming, and some of those reasons may be justified or socially acceptable whereas others may be unjustified or socially unacceptable. For example, a superhero may engage in multiple acts of violence against a villain in an effort to "save the world." The hero's violent actions seem legitimate or "justified" attempts to overcome the forces of evil. However, a serial killer may be shown murdering innocent, vulnerable, and helpless victims. Surely, the serial killer's violent actions are "unjustified" or socially unacceptable.

Research has consistently documented that seemingly justified portrayals of violence increase aggressive responding in both adult and child viewers (Berkowitz & Geen, 1967; Berkowitz & Powers, 1979; Geen & Stonner, 1973, 1974; Liss et al., 1983; Meyer, 1972). Scholars have argued that exposure to such portrayals reduces viewers' inhibitions toward aggressive responding (Jo & Berkowitz, 1994). Unjustified violence, on the other hand, has been found to have the exact opposite effect. That is, unjustified violence has been found to decrease aggressive responding in audience members (Berkowitz & Powers, 1979; Geen, 1981).

The fourth contextual feature is the presence of weapons. A variety of weapons may be used in violent portrayals. For example, a perpetrator of violence may use his or her natural means to overcome an enemy. Or, a police officer may fire his gun to "protect and serve" society. Other characters involved with violence may use explosives or heavy weaponry to annihilate their enemies. And still others may use unconventional weapons such as bats, ropes, chains, ice picks, or barbecue skewers to inflict physical harm. All of these examples illustrate the different types of weapons that may be used in a violent depiction.

What impact do violent portrayals featuring weapons have on viewers? Studies show that the presence of conventional weapons such as guns or knives significantly increases viewers' aggressive responding (Berkowitz & Le Page, 1967; Carlson, Marcus-Newhall, & Miller, 1990; Leyens & Parke, 1974; Page & O'Neal, 1977; Turner, Layton, & Simons, 1975). From a priming effects perspective, Berkowitz and others have argued that such weapons prompt or trigger aggressive thoughts and memories in viewers (Berkowitz, 1990; Leyens & Parke, 1974; Wilson et al.,

1996). When these types of thoughts are primed, viewers may be more susceptible to acting or behaving aggressively.

The fifth contextual feature is the extent and graphicness of violence. *Extent* refers not only to the duration or amount of time devoted to violence but also the distance with which such actions are portrayed. For example, a perpetrator may fire a gun from a long camera shot that lasts only for a split second. Or, a violent villain may engage in rapid fire that endures for several moments and encompasses the full frame of the TV screen. *Graphicness of violence*, on the other hand, refers to the amount of blood and carnage shown. Some violent scenes may not contain any blood or gore, whereas others may be bathed with such viscera.

Most of the research on extensive or graphic violence has focused on individuals' emotional desensitization to such portrayals. Several studies have found that both adult and child viewers become physiologically desensitized during exposure to violent programs or films (Cline, Croft, & Courrier, 1973; Lazarus & Alfert, 1964; Lazarus, Speisman, Mordkoff, & Davidson, 1962; Speisman, Lazarus, Mordkoff, & Davison, 1964). Other studies have examined individuals' emotional desensitization to violent programming over several viewing sessions, however.

Over the course of 2 weeks, Linz, Donnerstein, and Penrod (1988) exposed male study participants to five different "slasher films" (e.g., *Texas Chainsaw Massacre, Friday the 13th Part 2*). Participants' emotional reactions, perceptions of violence, and attitudes towards the female victims of violence in the film were assessed after each viewing session. After repeated exposure, subjects not only rated the films as less violent but also evaluated the film as less degrading to women (Wilson et al., 1996, p. 21). Similar findings have been replicated very recently by Mullin and Linz (1995). Taken together, these investigations indicate that both short- and long-term exposure to repeated acts of violence may contribute to viewers becoming emotionally desensitized to real-world aggression and its harmful physical, emotional, and psychological effects.

The sixth contextual variable is the realism of the violence. *Realism* refers to the actuality of the characters, settings, and events in violent portrayals. Some violent acts are portrayed as very realistic whereas others are depicted as completely fictional or fantastic in nature. Comparing the violence in *ABC Nightly News* with those aggressive actions in a Looney Tunes cartoon illustrates this difference.

Research has indicated that the level of realism surrounding a violent portrayal influences both aggressive responding and fear. In terms of

aggressive actions, several studies have found that more realistic portrayals of violence increase aggressive responding in children and
adult males significantly more than do fictionalized or fantastic
accounts of such behavior (Atkin, 1983; Berkowitz & Alioto, 1973;
Feshbach, 1972; Geen, 1975; Hapkiewicz & Stone, 1974; Thomas & Tell,
1974). Many scholars have argued that realistic depictions increase
aggressive responding for two reasons: (a) viewers can easily identify
with realistic perpetrators of violence, and (b) they may reduce viewers' inhibitions towards aggressive responding because they are so similar to real life (Jo & Berkowitz, 1994; Wilson et al., 1996[94], p. 23).

In terms of fear, several investigations have found realistic portrayals
of violence to be more emotionally disturbing or frightening to viewers
than fantastic depictions of aggression (Cantor & Sparks, 1984; Geen,
1975; Geen & Rakosky, 1975; Lazarus, Opton, Nomikos, & Rankin,
1965; Sparks, 1986). This effect has been documented with both children and adults.

Rewards and punishments are the seventh contextual element of violent portrayals. Rewards are those positive reinforcements that are
given to a perpetrator for acting violently. A perpetrator's reward for
violence may be as extravagant as $1,000,000 or as simple as a congrat-
ulatory pat on the back. Punishments, on the other hand, are those negative reinforcements that are given to a perpetrator for acting
aggressively. A perpetrator's punishment for violence may range from
a disapproving frown to the death penalty.

What impact do these types of positive and negative reinforcements
have on viewers? Research has indicated a powerful one. Studies have
found consistently that violence that is rewarded increases the risk of
learning aggressive thoughts and behaviors in both children and adults
(Bandura, Ross, & Ross, 1961, 1963b; Lando & Donnerstein, 1978).
Violence does not have to be explicitly rewarded to increase the risk of
a harmful effect, however. Social learning theory indicates that behavior that is not punished may also function as a tacit reward (Bandura,
1965; Walters & Parke, 1964). Thus, violence that is either rewarded or
not punished may facilitate viewers' learning of aggressive thoughts
and behaviors.

The eighth contextual feature is the consequences of violence.
Consequences refer to the harm and pain that occurs as a result of violence. For example, a target could let out a blood-curdling scream while
being stabbed with a knife. Such a reaction indicates that the target is
experiencing excruciating pain. Another character, however, may get

punched in the face and not even flinch. This response suggests that the character did not experience any pain or harm from the aggressive action.

Innumerable studies with adults have documented that intense harm and pain cues decrease aggressive responding in viewers (Baron 1971a, 1971b; Goransen, 1969; Sanders & Baron, 1975; Schmutte & Taylor, 1980). Many have argued that these types of cues inhibit aggressive responding because they "sensitize" viewers to the physical, emotional, and psychological harm that results from violence. To date, only one study has been conducted on children's responses to violent portrayals featuring harm and pain. Wotring and Greenberg (1973) found that young boys who were exposed to a violent clip depicting serious injuries were significantly less aggressive than those boys who saw an excerpt without any such injuries.

A handful of studies, however, have found harm and pain cues to increase aggressive behavior in viewers (Baron, 1979; Dubanoski & Kong, 1977; Swart & Berkowitz, 1976). These effects have been limited to either extremely angered study participants or participants who were highly susceptible to aggression and then placed in settings with aggressive cues in the environment (Wilson et al., 1996). In sum, the results from these studies suggest the depiction of physical pain or suffering functions as an inhibitor to aggressive responding for most viewers.

The ninth and last contextual feature is humor. Humor may be used in a myriad of ways in violent programming. For instance, a perpetrator may crack a joke immediately before, during, or after killing an innocent victim. Or, a violent act may be depicted in a farcical fashion. Alternatively, the consequences of violence may be presented in a comical and mirth-provoking manner. Clearly, these examples illuminate the heterogeneity of humor used in violent programming.

To date, we know very little about the impact of violent portrayals that feature humor. Indirect evidence has suggested, however, that humor may foster emotional desensitization. Studies have found that programs featuring high levels of humor are perceived as significantly less serious and less violent than those programs featuring low levels of humor (Gunter, 1985; Gunter & Furnham, 1984). Many scholars have speculated that humor trivializes the seriousness of violence (Wilson et al., 1996). Repeated exposure to trivialized violence may cause viewers to become desensitized or calloused towards violence and its real-world physical, emotional, and psychological harm.

Other studies have suggested, however, that violent portrayals flavored with humor may facilitate aggressive responding. That is, two studies have found that humor, when presented in a hostile context, increases aggressive behavior (Baron, 1978; Berkowitz, 1970). Many scholars have argued that humor may function as a reward or positive reinforcement for violence (Berkowitz, 1970; Wilson et al., 1996). As noted above, rewarded violence increases the risk of aggressive responding (Bandura, Ross, & Ross, 1961, 1963b; Lando & Donnerstein, 1978). Other scholars have suggested that humor may increase a viewer's level of arousal over that attained by violence alone (Wilson et al., 1996). Increased arousal has been found to increase aggressive responding (Zillmann, 1979). Taken together, these studies suggest that violent portrayals featuring humor may increase the risk of desensitization and aggressive behavior in viewers.

Clearly, all of the studies reviewed above indicate that the context within which violence is portrayed may increase or decrease the risk of aggression, desensitization, or fear in viewers. What these studies do not inform us about, however, is the particular contextual cues that pose the greatest risk to viewers. Are violent scenes featuring attractive perpetrators more problematic than those containing rewarded aggression? Do violent interactions portraying justified aggression pose a greater risk to viewers than those interactions involving conventional weapons? Nor do these studies illuminate the impact of violent scenes that contain several different contextual cues. For example, how are viewers affected by violent scenes featuring unattractive perpetrators engaging in justified and rewarded violence? Unequivocally, more research is needed in all of these areas.

Are There Any Solutions to the Problems Raised by Viewing Media Violence?

In considering the solutions to the problem of media violence, there are three major possibilities. The first is a legal remedy through governmental legislation. The second solution is education, primarily through teaching viewers media literacy and critical viewing skills. And the third solution is the development of media-initiated interventions such as public service announcements and entertainment programs designed specifically to deal with issues of violence. We will briefly examine each of these three possibilities and highlight those aspects most relevant to psychology.

Legal Solutions

In early 1996, the United States Congress passed a major telecommunications bill. One important component of this bill was the passage of a V-chip provision. This provision would require the broadcast industry to create a rating system for violence (and sex), and television manufacturers to build sets with blocking technology that would "automatically" turn off programs with a particular rating selected by an individual (i.e., a parent). The rating system supposedly would be based on the suitability of the program for children, using scales for violence, sexual content, and offensive language. Each show could transmit the rating with an electronic code that could be read by all new televisions 13 inches and over that would be required to have the V-chip technology.

On February 29, 1996, the president of the United States met with leaders in the entertainment industry who promised that within one year they would initiate an industry-wide rating system. This rating system would be based on an already existing rating system developed by the Motion Picture Association of America (MPAA). Although not directly duplicating the MPAA system, it would incorporate many of its components. There are, however, a number of potential problems with the already-existing MPAA rating system that need to be considered in light of a decision to use a variant of this system for the rating of violent television programs in the United States (i.e., Wilson, Linz, & Randall, 1990).

In their review of the MPAA system, Wilson and her colleagues noted three concerns with this rating scheme. First, the system attempts to rate films on the basis of what has been traditionally considered offensive rather than what is assumed to be or known to be "harmful" to viewers. The MPAA has asserted that it is concerned with attempting to determine what "most American parents will think about the appropriateness of film content" (Valenti, 1987, p. 5). The assumption that ratings should be based on what is offensive to parents rather than on what is assumed to be or known to be "harmful" to children often leads to peculiar classifications that ignore psychological facts and may ultimately not be all that informative to parents. For example, the scheme does not explicitly consider graphic horror as part of its criteria for rating films, in spite of the fact that numerous studies show that such content can cause intense emotional reactions in young viewers (see Wilson et al., 1990, for review).

Second, the system assumes that excessive and explicit sex is more offensive and problematic than excessive violence. According to the ratings board's guidelines, any depiction of sexuality will automatically render a film an R rating, and explicit sex will often earn a film an X rating. In contrast, a film can contain violence and still be given a G, PG, or PG-13 rating. The rule of thumb is that the violence must be "rough" or "persistent" before a film will receive an R rating, and "excessive and sadistic" before a film will warrant an X rating. In most cases, however, films that contain graphic and brutal violence are assigned R ratings even when the violence is directed against women in an erotic context (e.g., slasher films). As an illustration of these differential standards regarding sex and violence, the film *The French Lieutenant's Woman* is rated R because of sexual references and a few brief sex scenes, whereas a film such as *Conan the Destroyer* is rated PG despite scenes of "bloodthirsty battlers at every turn" (Martin & Porter, 1987, p. 1049).

Third, the ratings system presumes that films should be rated primarily on the basis of the amount of violence and sex, or the explicitness of such content, rather than on the context in which these depictions occur. Little attention appears to be given to contextual features of the violence, such as how realistic it is, the rewards and punishments associated with the violent act, and the degree of justification for the violence. The same approach is applied to depictions of sex. The Board appears to pay little attention to motives of the character or other features of the situation in which the sexual contact takes place. Consequently, movies containing depictions of rape and sexual brutality seem to receive the same ratings as movies depicting mutually affectionate lovemaking, so long as they both contain the same amount of sexual activity. Moreover, the ratings board has a policy that two or more uses of a sexually derived word as an expletive in a film will earn it an R rating. As a result, a movie like *Rainman*, which depicts the growing relationship between a man and his autistic brother, receives the same rating (R) as the so-called "slasher" films that gratuitously depict violence against women.

A few years ago the MPAA attempted to respond to some of its critics by creating the "NC-17" (i.e., no children under 17) rating to warn viewers about content that may include "adult" themes that are not necessarily deemed pornographic. Interestingly, this change coincided with strong pressure from influential film producers who objected to the X rating as a label for films that are somewhat sexually explicit but that deal with a serious topic. The addition of another rating category does not, however, address the more deep-seated problems. More fundamental changes in the system are necessary before these issues can be resolved. It has been argued elsewhere that both the age specifications and the actual ratings need to be more informative to parents (Wilson et al., 1990). An alternative scheme could be based on the same two factors used by the MPAA: age level and type of film content. However, the categories of film content need to specify the precise type of content in a film and the most vulnerable age groups. For example, a slasher film such as *Toolbox Murders* might be labeled "SV: 13–17," suggesting that it contains sexual violence or violence in the context of sexual depictions, and that it is particularly unsuitable for 13- to 17-year-olds, but also not appropriate for younger children.

Suggestions for revising the rating system made by Wilson, Linz, and Randall (1990) were recently adopted by the American Psychological Association's Commission on Youth and Violence. The APA made the following recommendation:

> The Film Rating System should be reexamined with an emphasis toward that which is "harmful" to children rather than that which might be offensive to parents. A stronger consideration needs to be placed upon violent and sexually violent content in the assignment of ratings, as well as providing for the viewer more information on the kind and scope of violence present. (Donnerstein, Slaby, & Eron, 1994, p. 246)

Along these same lines, the video rental market needs to be more in harmony with even the present rating system. Easy access by young adolescents to R-rated graphically violent videos undermines the meaning of the R rating. This rating indicates that children under 17 are "restricted" from such films unless accompanied by a parent or guardian. Such restrictions are rather uncommon within the video market (Donnerstein, Slaby, & Eron, 1994, p. 240).

Critical Viewing

As an alternative to regulation, a large number of organizations concerned with the well-being of children and families have recommended that professionals take a more active role in reducing the impact of violent media (American Academy of Pediatrics, American Medical Association, American Psychological Association, Group for the Advancement of Psychiatry, National Parent Teachers Association).

Research on intervention programs has indicated that we can reduce some of the impact of media violence by "empowering" parents in their roles as monitors of children's television viewing.

Another strategy has been to provide child viewers themselves with the cognitive tools necessary to resist the influence of television violence. A number of programs have been designed to build "critical viewing skills" that may ameliorate the impact of television violence on younger viewers. The effectiveness of these programs is still under evaluation. Curricula are designed to teach students to recognize certain types of negative portrayals of social behavior and to provide them with alternative ways of interpreting these portrayals. Others have speculated that the effects of exposure to certain mass communications could be modified if a viewer has the ability to devalue the source of information, to assess motivations for presenting information, and to perceive the degree of reality intended.

Some of the techniques discussed above have been applied to interventions designed to mitigate the impact of exposure to mass media sexual violence. Linz, Wilson, and Donnerstein (1992) have suggested that a systematic program of research whose goal is the development of a formal, easily administered educational program concerning sexual violence in the media be undertaken. The program should be suitable for high school educators. To create such a program, research is needed to examine what types of information would be most powerful in changing adolescents' attitudes about sexual violence in mass media, the optimal format for adolescents to learn and incorporate these messages into their repertoire of values, the most effective communication source for conveying this educational information, and whether social psychological factors, such as a critical viewing companion, facilitate immediate and long-term changes in beliefs and attitudes about sexual violence. It is believed that this and other educational interventions will be effective to the extent that they are formed and administered on the basis of systematic research into each of these questions.

In summary, the research evidence to date is consistent with a call for more educational interventions. Along with media literacy programs, efforts in entertainment broadcasts to educate viewers about violence in society, including media violence, might also be effective. Our ever-increasing knowledge of media effects, attitude formation and change, child development, and human behavior suggests that this is an effective means to deal with the problem of violence in our society.

Media Initiated Interventions

Another educational resource is the mass media itself. Educational movies about violence, that are written, designed, and professionally produced to be entertaining have great potential for informing the public and, under some conditions, might even change antisocial attitudes about violence. Research evaluating the impact of antismoking television information spots, for example, has demonstrated that these messages have been successful in increasing public awareness about the negative health consequences of smoking (Flay, 1986). However, this success presumably has been the result of the large number of antismoking messages delivered during popular viewing times. Many public service announcements do not produce significant effects because the campaigns consist of a small number of spots, often of questionable quality, that are delivered during nonprime viewing hours (Flay & Cook, 1989). In order for these types of programs to be effective, they must be viewed by a large proportion of the population.

As an example of entertainment programming that can influence individuals' attitudes, the National Broadcast Company (NBC) aired several made for television movies designed to inform, as well as entertain viewers about the problem of acquaintance or date rape. In September of 1990, NBC aired a made-for-TV movie about the trauma and aftermath of acquaintance rape. This program, titled *She Said No*, was featured during prime-time hours and attracted a large viewing audience. In spite of competitive programming on other stations, the movie earned a Nielsen rating of 14.7, indicating that the program was seen in more than 13 million households. These audience statistics suggest that the movie was entertaining despite its prosocial, anti rape-myth message. *She Said No* also received critical acclaim, winning an award from American Women in Radio and Television (AWRT) for its realistic portrayal of the plight of a rape victim.

An evaluation of the effectiveness of this movie was undertaken by Wilson, Linz, Donnerstein, and Stipp (1992). The study measured audience responses to the program. Specifically, Wilson and her colleagues examined whether exposure to this movie would decrease acceptance of rape myths or increase awareness of date rape as a serious social problem. Unlike many of the intervention projects discussed in this chapter, this study possessed both high external *and* internal validity. First, the study used a nationally representative sample of adults in the United States. This permitted generalization of the findings to a broad range of American viewers. Second, individuals from this representative sample were randomly assigned to view or not view the made-for-TV movie. This allowed cause-and-effect conclusions to be drawn. Third, subjects viewed the television movie in their own home—a more natural viewing environment than is achieved in most media experiments.

A total of 1,038 adults, randomly selected from four locations in the United States, were assigned to view over a closed-circuit channel, or not to view, *She Said No* prior to the network broadcast of the film. The viewers and nonviewers were contacted the next day and asked about acceptance of rape myths and perceptions of rape as a social problem. The results of this study indicated that the television movie was a useful tool in educating and altering perceptions about date rape. Specifically, exposure to the movie increased awareness of date rape as a social problem across all viewers. The movie also had a prosocial effect on older women, who were less likely to attribute blame to women in date rape situations after exposure to the movie.

Three possible solutions to the problems with media violence in America have been presented: governmental legislation, educational initiatives, and media-based entertainment campaigns. Each of these solutions, either independently or interactively, may help to mitigate some of the potential harm that media violence poses to viewers.

Conclusion

Overall, we may conclude that the mass media contribute to a number of antisocial effects in both children and adults. We must keep in mind, however, that the mass media are but one factor, which may not even be the most important factor, that contributes to antisocial attitudes and behaviors in individuals. Furthermore, the mass media's impact can be mitigated and/or controlled with reasonable insight. We have discussed a number of ways in which the media, parents, and others can be used to prevent antisocial effects of exposure to violent mass media fare.

A few years ago at an address to members of the entertainment industry, Senator Paul Simon (1993), who has been actively involved in the TV violence debate, noted, "This is no longer theory. The evidence that television violence does harm is now just as overwhelming as the

evidence that cigarettes do harm." At this address he made seven suggestions to members of the entertainment industry on what he believed
needed to be done regarding the issue of media violence. First, he
argued that there should be recognition by the creative community that
self-restraint is essential for a democracy to function. According to
Simon, "The best way to protect your industry from the dangerous and
heavy hand of government is to exercise self-restraint. The gauge of
whether we are a civilized society is not to what extremes we can
indulge ourselves." Second, the entire industry needs to be involved in
self-restraint, including cable, film, and independents. Third, there
needs to be a continuity of effort and concern in this area. In this regard,
Simon called for an ongoing monitoring of TV violence on both network and cable programming. And, he suggested the possibility of an
Advisory Office on Television Violence so that there will be a continuing effort among the industry to deal effectively with the violence issue.
As Simon noted, "if within the industry you do not exercise self-
restraint, neither will many of those who are concerned. Extremes in
behavior invite extremes in response."

Fourth, he suggested that glamorized violence should be avoided
and the harmful effects of violence need to be presented. Simon also
added that it is important for the industry to begin considering nonviolent solutions to conflict in their dramatic presentations. The concern
over violent promotions was Simon's fifth issue. He suggested that
such promotions be reduced and that during times when children are
in the audience they be eliminated. Sixth was the suggestion that the
television medium should be used to educate the public about the
harmful effects of violence, particularly media violence. Seventh and
last, Simon wanted to remind the audience of the international impact
of the American media. As he noted when discussing concerns that
other countries had with violence in the American media, "The revul-
sion in many nations to parts of the American culture is not a reaction
to the Chicago Symphony Orchestra . . . nor is it in response to our finer
movies or television shows. We should ask ourselves what messages
we wish to send to other nations." In total, Senator Simon's message
was clear: There is too much violence on television and something
needs to be done.

In these last few years we have seen a great deal of response to
Senator Simon's suggestions. We expect that the debate, solutions, and
concerns will continue in the years ahead, and that the psychological
community will be deeply involved at all these levels.

REFERENCES

American Psychological Association. (1993). *Violence and youth: Psychology's response*. Washington, DC: Author.

Atkin, C. (1983). Effects of realistic TV violence vs. fictional violence on aggression. *Journalism Quarterly, 60*, 615–621.

Bandura, A. (1965). Influence of models' reinforcement contingencies on the acquisition of imitative responses. *Journal of Personality and Social Psychology, 1*(6), 589–595.

Bandura, A. (1971). *Social learning theory*. New York: General Learning Press.

Bandura, A. (1986). *Social foundations of thought and action: A social cognitive theory*. Englewood Cliffs, NJ: Prentice-Hall.

Bandura, A. (1994). Social cognitive theory of mass communication. In J. Bryant & D. Zillmann (Eds.), *Media effects* (pp. 61–90). Hillsdale, NJ: Erlbaum.

Bandura, A., Ross, D., & Ross, S. A. (1961). Transmission of aggression through imitation of aggressive models. *Journal of Abnormal and Social Psychology, 63*, 575–582.

Bandura, A., Ross, D., & Ross, S. A. (1963a). Imitation of film-mediated aggressive models. *Journal of Abnormal and Social Psychology, 66*, 3–11.

Bandura, A., Ross, D., & Ross, S. A. (1963b). Vicarious reinforcement and imitative learning. *Journal of Abnormal and Social Psychology, 67*, 601–607.

Baron, R. A. (1971a). Aggression as a function of magnitude of victim's pain cues, level of prior anger arousal, and aggressor-victim similarity. *Journal of Personality and Social Psychology, 18*(1), 48–54.

Baron, R. A. (1971b). Magnitude of victim's pain cues and level of prior anger arousal as determinants of adult aggressive behavior. *Journal of Personality and Social Psychology, 17*(3), 236–243.

Baron, R. A. (1978). The influence of hostile and nonhostile humor upon physical aggression. *Personality and Social Psychology Bulletin, 4*(1), 77–80.

Baron, R. A. (1979). Effects of victim's pain cues, victim's race, and level of prior instigation upon physical aggression. *Journal of Applied Social Psychology, 9*(2), 103–114.

Berkowitz, L. (1970). Aggressive humor as a stimulus to aggressive responses. *Journal of Personality and Social Psychology, 16*(4), 710–717.

Berkowitz, L. (1973). Words and symbols as stimuli to aggressive responses. In J. Knutson (Ed.), *Control of aggression: Implications from basic research*. Chicago: Aldine-Atherton.

Berkowitz, L. (1984). Some effects of thoughts on anti- and prosocial influences of media events: A cognitive-neoassociation analysis. *Psychological Bulletin, 95*(3), 410–427.

Berkowitz, L. (1990). On the formation and regulation of anger and aggression: A cognitive neoassociationistic analysis. *American Psychologist, 45*(4), 494–503.

Berkowitz, L., & Alioto, J. T. (1973). The meaning of an observed event as a determinant of its aggressive consequences. *Journal of Personality and Social Psychology, 28*(2), 206–217.

Berkowitz, L., & Geen, R. G. (1967). Stimulus qualities of the target of aggression: A further study. *Journal of Personality and Social Psychology, 5*(3), 364–368.

Berkowitz, L., & LePage, A. (1967). Weapons as aggression-eliciting stimuli. *Journal of Personality and Social Psychology, 7*(2), 202–207.

Berkowitz, L., & Powers, P. C. (1979). Effects of timing and justification of witnessed aggression on the observers' punitiveness. *Journal of Research in Personality, 13,* 71–80.

Berkowitz, L., & Rogers, K. H. (1986). A priming effect analysis of media influences. In J. Bryant & D. Zillmann (Eds.), *Perspectives on media effects* (pp. 57–82). Hillsdale, NJ: Erlbaum.

Cantor, J. (1994). Fright reactions to mass media. In J. Bryant & D. Zillmann (Eds.), *Media effects* (pp. 213–245). Hillsdale, NJ: Erlbaum.

Cantor, J., & Sparks, G. G. (1984). Children's fear responses to mass media: Testing some Piagetian predictions. *Journal of Communication, 34*(2), 90–103.

Cantor, J., & Wilson, B. J. (1988). Helping children cope with frightening media presentations. *Current Psychology: Research & Reviews, 7,* 58–75.

Carlson, M., Marcus-Newhall, A., & Miller, N. (1990). Effects of situational aggression cues: A quantitative review. *Journal of Personality and Social Psychology, 58*(4), 622–633.

Carver, C. S., Ganellen, R. J., Froming, W. J., & Chambers, W. (1983). Modeling: An analysis in terms of category accessibility. *Journal of Experimental Social Psychology, 19,* 403–421.

Centers for Disease Control and Prevention. (1991). *Position papers from the Third National Injury Conference: Setting the National Agenda for Injury Control in the 1990s.* Washington, DC: U.S. Department of Health and Human Services.

Children Now. (1995, November). *Sending Signals: Kids speak out about values in the media.* Sacramento, CA: Author. (Also available E-mail: Children@dnai.com)

Cline, V. B., Croft, R. G., & Courrier, S. (1973). Desensitization of children to television violence. *Journal of Personality and Social Psychology, 27*(3), 360–365.

Comisky, P., & Bryant, J. (1982). Factors involved in generating suspense. *Human Communication Research, 9*(1), 49–58.

Comstock, G., & Paik, H. (1991). *Television and the American child.* New York: Academic Press.

Donnerstein, E., Slaby, R., & Eron, L. (1994). The mass media and youth aggression. In L. D. Eron, J. H. Gentry, & P. Schlegel (Eds.), *A reason to hope: A psychosocial perspective on violence and youth* (pp. 217–250). Washington, DC: American Psychological Association.

Dubanoski, R. A., & Kong, C. (1977). The effects of pain cues on the behavior of high and low aggressive boys. *Social Behavior and Personality, 5*(2), 273–279.

Eron, L. D., Gentry, J. H., & Schlegel, P. (1994). *Reason to hope: A psychosocial perspective on violence & youth*. Washington, DC: American Psychological Association.

Feshbach, N. D., & Roe, K. (1968). Empathy in six- and seven-year-olds. *Child Development, 39*(1), 133–145.

Feshbach, S. (1972). Reality and fantasy in filmed violence. In J. P. Murray, E. A. Rubinstein, & G. Comstock (Eds.), *Television and social behavior: Television and social learning* (Vol. 2, pp. 318–345). Washington, DC: U.S. Government Printing Office.

Flay, B. R. (1986, May). Mass media and smoking cessation. Paper presented at the annual meeting of the International Communication Association, Chicago.

Flay, B. R., & Cook, T. D. (1989). Three models for summative evaluation of prevention campaigns with a mass media component. In R. E. Rice & C. A. Atkin (Eds.), *Public communication campaigns* (2nd ed., pp. 175–200). Newbury Park, CA: Sage.

Foa, E. B., & Kozak, M. J. (1986). Emotional processing of fear: Exposure to corrective information. *Psychological Bulletin, 99*, 20–35.

Geen, R. G. (1975). The meaning of observed violence: Real vs. fictional violence and consequent effects on aggression and emotional arousal. *Journal of Research In Personality, 9*, 270–281.

Geen, R. G. (1981). Behavioral and physiological reactions to observed violence: Effects of prior exposure to aggressive stimuli. *Journal of Personality and Social Psychology, 40*(5), 868–875.

Geen, R. G., & Rakosky, J. J. (1975). Interpretations of observed violence and their effects on GSR. *Journal of Experimental Research in Personality, 6*, 289–292.

Geen, R. G., & Stonner, D. (1973). Context effects in observed violence. *Journal of Personality and Social Psychology, 25*(1), 145–150.

Geen, R. G., & Stonner, D. (1974). The meaning of observed violence: Effects on arousal and aggressive behavior. *Journal of Research in Personality, 8*, 55–63.

Gerbner, G. (1969). Dimensions of violence in television drama. In R. K. Baker & S. J. Ball (Eds.), *Violence in the media* (Staff Report to the National Commission on the Causes and Prevention of Violence, pp. 311–340). Washington, DC: U.S. Government Printing Office.

Gerbner, G. (1992, December). Testimony at Hearings on Violence on Television before the House Judiciary Committee, Subcommittee on Crime and Criminal Justice, New York (field hearing).

Gerbner, G., & Gross, L. (1976). Living with television: The violence profile. *Journal of Communication, 26*(2), 172–199.

Gerbner, G., Gross, L., Morgan, M., & Signorielli, N. (1994). Growing up with television: The cultivation perspective. In J. Bryant & D. Zillmann (Eds.), *Media effects* (pp. 17–41). Hillsdale, NJ: Erlbaum.

Gerbner, G., Gross, L., Signorielli, N. & Morgan, M. (1986). Living with television: The dynamics of the cultivation process. In J. Bryant & D. Zillmann (Eds.), *Perspectives on media effects* (pp. 17–40). Hillsdale, NJ: Erlbaum.

Gerbner, G., & Signorielli, N. (1990). *Violence profile, 1967 through 1988–89: Enduring patterns*. Unpublished manuscript, Annenberg School of Communication, University of Pennsylvania, Philadelphia.

Goransen, R. E. (1969). Observed violence and aggressive behavior: The effects of negative outcomes to observed violence. *Dissertation Abstracts International, 31*(01), DAI-B. (University Microfilms No. AAC77 08286)

Gunter, B. (1985). *Dimensions of television violence.* Aldershots, England: Gower.

Gunter, B. (1994). The question of media violence. In J. Bryant & D. Zillmann (Eds.), *Media effects* (pp. 163–211). Hillsdale, NJ: Erlbaum.

Gunter, B., & Furnham, A. (1984). Perceptions of television violence: Effects of programme genre and physical forms of violence. *British Journal of Social Psychology, 23*, 155–184.

Hapkiewicz, W. G., & Stone, R. D. (1974). The effect of realistic versus imaginary aggressive models on children's interpersonal play. *Child Study Journal, 4*(2), 47–58.

Harris, R. J. (1994). The impact of sexually explicit media. In J. Bryant & D. Zillmann (Eds.), *Media effects* (pp. 247–272). Hillsdale, NJ: Erlbaum.

Huesmann, L. R. (1986). Psychological processes promoting the relation between exposure to media violence and aggressive behavior by the viewer. *Journal of Social Issues, 42*(3), 125–140.

Huesmann, L. R. (1992, March). *Violence in the mass media.* Paper presented at the Third International Conference on Film Regulation, London, England.

Huesmann, L. R., & Eron, L. D. (Eds.). (1986). *Television and the aggressive child: A cross-national comparison.* Hillsdale, NJ: Erlbaum.

Huesmann, L. R., Eron, L. D., Lefkowitz, M. M., & Walder, L. O. (1984). The stability of aggression over time and generations. *Developmental Psychology, 20*, 1120–1134.

Huesmann, L. R., Lagerspetz, K., & Eron, L. D. (1984). Intervening variables in the TV violence-aggression relation: Evidence from two countries. *Developmental Psychology, 20*, 1120–1134.

Huston, A. C., Donnerstein, E., Fairchild, H., Feshbach, N. D., Katz, P. A., Murray, J. P., Rubinstein, E. A., Wilcox, B. L., & Zuckerman, D. (1992). *Big world, small screen: The role of television in American society.* Lincoln: University of Nebraska Press.

Jo, E., & Berkowitz, L. (1994). A priming effect analysis of media influences: An update. In J. Bryant & D. Zillmann (Eds.), *Media effects* (pp. 43–60). Hillsdale, NJ: Erlbaum.

Jose, P. E., & Brewer, W. F. (1984). Development of story liking: Character identification, suspense, and outcome resolution. *Developmental Psychology, 20*, 911–924.

Kubey, R. W., & Csikszentmihalyi, M. (1990). *Television and the quality of life: How viewing shapes everyday experience.* Hillsdale, NJ: Erlbaum.

Lando, H. A., & Donnerstein, E. I. (1978). The effects of a model's success or failure on subsequent aggressive behavior. *Journal of Research In Personality, 12*, 225–234.

Lazarus, R. S., & Alfert, E. (1964). Short-circuiting of threat by experimentally altering cognitive appraisal. *Journal of Abnormal and Social Psychology, 69*(2), 195–205.

Lazarus, R. S., Opton, E. M., Nomikos, M. S., & Rankin, N. O. (1965). The principal of short-circuiting of threat: Further evidence. *Journal of Personality, 33*, 622–635.

Lazarus, R. S., Speisman, M., Mordkoff, A. M., & Davidson, L. A. (1962). A laboratory study of psychological stress produced by a motion picture film. *Psychological Monographs: General and Applied, 76*(34 Whole No. 553).

Lefkowitz, M. M., Eron, L. D., Walder, L. Q., & Huesmann, L. R. (1977). *Growing up to be violent: A longitudinal study of the development of aggression.* New York: Pergamon Press.

Leyens, J. P., & Parke, R. D. (1974). Aggressive slides can induce a weapons effect. *European Journal of Social Psychology, 5*(2), 229–236.

Leyens, J. P., & Picus, S. (1973). Identification with the winner of a fight and name mediation: Their differential effects upon subsequent aggressive behavior. *British Journal of Social and Clinical Psychology, 12,* 374–377.

Lichter, S. R., & Amundson, D. (1992). *A day of television violence.* Washington, DC: Center for Media and Public Affairs.

Liebert, R. M., & Baron, R. A. (1972). Short-term effects of televised aggression on children's aggressive behavior. In J. P. Murray, E. A. Rubenstein, & G. A. Comstock (Eds.), *Television and social behavior: Television and social learning* (Vol. 2, pp. 181–201). Washington, DC: U.S. Government Printing Office.

Linz, D., & Donnerstein, E. (1994). Sex and violence in slasher films: A reinterpretation. *Journal of Broadcasting & Electronic Media, 38*(2), 243–246.

Linz, D., Donnerstein, E., & Penrod, S. (1984). The effects of multiple exposures to filmed violence against women. *Journal of Communication, 34*(3), 130–147.

Linz, D., Donnerstein, E., & Penrod, S. (1987). Sexual violence in the mass media: Social psychological implications. In P. Shaver & C. Hendrick (Eds.), *Review of personality and social psychology* (Vol. 7., pp. 95–123). Newbury Park, CA: Sage.

Linz, D. G., Donnerstein, E., & Penrod, S. (1988). Effects of long-term exposure to violent and sexually degrading depictions of women. *Journal of Personality and Social Psychology, 55*(5), 758–768.

Linz, D., Wilson, B. J., & Donnerstein, E. (1992). Sexual violence in the mass media: Legal solutions, warnings and mitigation through education. *Journal of Social Issues, 48*(1), 145–171.

Liss, M. B., Reinhardt, L. C., & Fredriksen, S. (1983). TV heroes: The impact of rhetoric and deeds. *Journal of Applied Developmental Psychology, 4,* 175–187.

Malamuth, N., & Check, J. V. P. (1981). The effects of mass media exposure on acceptance of violence against women: A field experiment. *Journal of Research in Personality, 15,* 436–446.

Martin, M., & Porter, M. (1987). *Video movie guide 1988.* New York: Ballantine Books.

Mathai, J. (1983). An acute anxiety state in an adolescent precipitated by viewing a horror movie. *Journal of Adolescence, 6,* 197–200.

Meyer, T. P. (1972). Effects of viewing justified and unjustified real film violence on aggressive behavior. *Journal of Personality and Social Psychology, 23*(1), 21–29.

Mullin, C. R., & Linz, D. (1995). Desensitization and resensitization to violence against women: Effects of exposure to sexually violent films on judgments of domestic violence victims. *Journal of Personality and Social Psychology, 69*(3), 449–459.

National Academy of Science. (1993). *Understanding and preventing violence.* Washington, DC: National Academy Press.

National Institute of Mental Health. (1982). *Television and behavior: Ten years of scientific progress and implications for the eighties (Vol. I). Summary Report.* Washington, DC: U.S. Government Printing Office.

National Television Violence Study. (1996). Violence in television programming overall: University of California, Santa Barbara. *Scientific Papers: National Television Violence Study* (pp. 1–172). Studio City, CA: Mediascope.

Neisser, U. (1967). *Cognitive psychology.* New York: Appleton-Century-Crofts.

Page, D., & O'Neal, E. (1977). "Weapons effect" without demand characteristics. *Psychological Reports, 41,* 29–30.

Paik, H., & Comstock, G. (1994). The effects of television violence on antisocial behavior: A meta-analysis. *Communication Research, 21*(4), 516–546.

Perry, D. G., & Perry, L. C. (1976). Identification with film characters, covert aggressive verbalization, and reactions to film violence. *Journal of Research in Personality, 10,* 399–409.

Potter, W. J. (1986). Perceived reality and the cultivation hypothesis. *Journal of Broadcasting & Electronic Media, 30*(2), 159–174.

Potter, W. J. (1993). Cultivation theory and research: A conceptual critique. *Human Communication Research, 19,* 564–601.

Rubin, A. M., Perse, E. M., & Taylor, D. S. (1988). A methodological examination of cultivation. *Communication Research, 15,* 107–134.

Sanders, G. S., & Baron, R. S. (1975). Pain cues and uncertainty as determinants of aggression in a situation involving repeated instigation. *Journal of Personality and Social Psychology, 32*(3), 495–502.

Schmutte, G. T., & Taylor, S. P. (1980). Physical aggression as a function of alcohol and pain feedback. *The Journal of Social Psychology, 110,* 235–244.

Shapiro, M. A. (1991). Memory and decision processes in the construction of social reality. *Communication Research, 18,* 3–24.

Simon, P. (1993, August 2). Remarks of United States Senator Paul Simon to the Television/film meeting on TV violence, Los Angeles.

Sparks, G. G. (1986). Developmental differences in children's reports of fear induced by the mass media. *Child Study Journal, 16,* 55–66.

Speisman, J. C., Lazarus, R. S., Mordkoff, A., & Davison, L. (1964). Experimental reduction of stress based on ego-defense theory. *Journal of Abnormal and Social Psychology, 68*(4), 367–380.

Surgeon General's Scientific Advisory Committee on Television and Social Behavior. (1972). *Television and growing up: The impact of televised violence.* Washington, DC: U.S. Government Printing Office.

Swart, C., & Berkowitz, L. (1976). Effects of a stimulus associated with a victim's pain on later aggression. *Journal of Personality and Social Psychology, 33*(5), 623–631.

Tan, A. S. (1986). Social learning of aggression from television. In J. Bryant & D. Zillmann (Eds.), *Perspectives on media effects* (pp. 41–55). Hillsdale, NJ: Erlbaum.

Tangey, J. P., & Feshbach, S. (1988). Children's television-viewing frequency: Individual differences and demographic correlates. *Personality and Social Psychology Bulletin, 14,* 145–158.

Thomas, M. H. (1982). Physiological arousal, exposure to a relatively lengthy aggressive film, and aggressive behavior. *Journal of Research in Personality, 16,* 72–81.

Thomas, M. H., Horton, R. W., Lippencott, E. C., & Drabman, R. S. (1977). Desensitization to portrayals of real-life aggression as a function of exposure to television violence. *Journal of Personality and Social Psychology, 35,* 450–458.

Thomas, M. H., & Tell, P. M. (1974). Effects of viewing real versus fantasy violence upon interpersonal aggression. *Journal of Research In Personality, 8,* 153–160.

Turner, C. W., & Berkowitz, L. (1972). Identification with film aggressor (covert role taking) and reactions to film violence. *Journal of Personality and Social Psychology, 21*(2), 256–264.

Turner, C. W., Layton, J. F., & Simons, L. S. (1975). Naturalistic studies of aggressive behavior: Aggressive stimuli, victim visibility, and horn honking. *Journal of Personality and Social Psychology, 31*(6), 1098–1107.

Valenti, J. (1987). *The voluntary movie rating system.* New York: Motion Picture Association of America.

Walters, R. H., & Parke, R. D. (1964). Influence of response consequences to a social model on resistance to deviation. *Journal of Experimental Child Psychology, 1,* 269–280.

Wilkins, W. (1971). Desensitization: Social cognitive factors underlying effectiveness of Wolpe's procedure. *Psychological Bulletin, 76,* 311–317.

Wilson, B. J. (1995). Les recherches sur médias et violence: Aggressivité, désensibilisation, peur [Effects of media violence: Aggression, desensitization, and fear]. *Les Cahiers de la Sécurité Intérieure, 20*(2), 21–37.

Wilson, B. J., & Cantor, J. (1985). Developmental differences in empathy with a television protagonist's fear. *Journal of Experimental Child Psychology, 39,* 284–299.

Wilson, B. J., Kunkel, D., Linz, D., Potter, W. J., Donnerstein, E., Smith, S. L., Blumenthal, E. Y., & Grey, T. E. (1996). Television violence and its context: A content analysis 1994–1995. *Executive summary: National television violence study* (pp. 8–30). Studio City, CA: Mediascope.

Wilson, B. J., Linz, D., & Randall, B. (1990). Applying social science research to film ratings: A shift from offensiveness to harmful effects. *Journal of Broadcasting and Electronic Media, 34,* 443–468.

Wilson, B. J., Linz, D., Donnerstein, E., & Stipp, H. (1992). The impact of social issue television programming on attitudes toward rape. *Human Communication Research, 19,* 179–208.

Worchel, S. (1972). The effect of films on the importance of behavioral freedom. *Journal of Personality, 40,* 417–435.

Wotring, C. E., & Greenberg, B. S. (1973). Experiments in televised violence and verbal aggression: Two exploratory studies. *The Journal of Communication, 23,* 446–460.

Zillmann, D. (1979). *Hostility and aggression.* Hillsdale, NJ: Erlbaum.

Zillmann, D. (1980). Anatomy of suspense. In P. H. Tannenbaum (Ed.), *The entertainment functions of television* (pp. 133–163). Hillsdale, NJ: Erlbaum.

Zillmann, D. (1982). Television viewing and arousal. In D. Pearl, L. Bouthilet, & J. Lazar (Eds.), *Television and behavior: Ten years of scientific progress and implications for the eighties* (Vol. 2, pp. 53–67). Washington, DC: U.S. Government Printing Office.

Zillmann, D. (1991). Empathy: Affect from bearing witness to the emotions of others. In J. Bryant & D. Zillmann (Eds.), *Responding to the screen* (pp. 135–167). Hillsdale, NJ: Erlbaum.

Zillmann, D., & Cantor, J. R. (1977). Affective responses to the emotions of a protagonist. *Journal of Experimental Social Psychology, 13,* 155–165.

3

Gender and Age in Prime-Time Television

George Gerbner

Humans grow up and live in a world erected by the stories we tell. The storytelling process of a culture functions to socialize children, to define their world and their roles, and to indicate their powers and risks. The most essential building blocks of this exercise in casting and fate are gender and age. And its most critical defining characteristic has been a historic transformation in the storytelling.

That transformation has occurred over the past 30 years. The shift has been marked by a trend away from stories being told mostly by parents, schools and churches, and other traditional socializing agencies toward stories being delivered by a group of highly concentrated and globalized corporate "content providers" who have things to sell. The mainstream of that process is television. Today's children are born into homes in which a television is on over 7 hours a day. Who is cast in what role and assigned what fate in the world of television sends the most pervasive messages to our children about life's values, rewards, penalties, and risks.

The most compelling part of that process, and the part that dominates early socialization, is prime-time dramatic programs. Unlike fragmented and opaque "facts," drama takes us behind the scenes and shows how things are supposed to work. It deals in coherent ways with key questions of existence: What is the world like? What is my role in it? How do I relate to others? What fate may be in store for me?

The typical child viewer sees each week about 353 characters in prime-time dramatic programs, both serious and humorous. Never before have children been so consistently exposed to such a range of human types and situations. That is the new context in which gender and aging as social roles are learned.

Although the fictional world of television is often realistic, it is never real but contrived, selective, and synthetic. Its overall patterns of casting and fate reflect the formulas of their production. Casting defines the types of characters who populate the world of television, fate defines their destiny.

This report is based on an analysis of 20 years (from 1973 through 1993) of prime-time major network dramatic entertainment programs (Gerbner, Gross, Morgan, & Signorielli, 1994). A brief note will summarize Saturday morning children's programming patterns that occupy approximately one fifth of a child's viewing time. Additional information comes from the Annenberg Script Archive, containing scripts of dramatic programs aired on television.

The study was conducted by the Cultural Indicators (CI) project research team under the direction of the author.[1] It was designed to reveal aggregate patterns of images and messages that large communities absorb over long periods of time. The annual samples consist of all dramatic programs and all speaking parts aired on the four networks (ABC, CBS, NBC, and Fox) for a typical week for each season. The samples were recorded and coded by a group of trained observers using an

---

[1] CI is an ongoing long-range research project that monitors television content and relates it to viewers' conceptions of reality. The project began at the University of Pennsylvania's The Annenberg School for Communication and continues at the University City Science Center in Philadelphia. Nejat Ozyegin has directed data processing. Coding supervisers and coordinators have been Elvira Arcenas, S. Marcus Hswe, Jennifer Luk, Ilicia Stangle, and Sheila Witherington. Leah Binder assisted with the special script analysis.

instrument of analysis and subjected to periodic reliability testing. All aggregate information comes from the CI database.

The samples included a total of 2,452 programs and 1,596 program hours. All speaking parts, a total of 30,952 characters, were analyzed (see Table 1). They are tabulated in two types of age categories. The first classification is under 18, 18–44, 45–64 ("midlife"), and 65 and over. When the focus on specific roles reduces the number of characters involved, the comparisons are made in two broader adult categories: "young," judged to be 18 through 44, and "midlife and older" (or just "older"), playing roles of 45 years and above. "Major characters," tabulated separately, are those judged to be essential to the plot.

Table 1

Programs, Program Hours, and Characters Analyzed

		Programs		
		Prime Time	Sat a.m.	Totals
Networks				
ABC		458	256	714
CBS		491	402	893
NBC		462	290	752
FOX		67	26	93
Total		1,478	974	2,452
Program hours				
ABC		387	86	473
CBS		440	107	547
NBC		434	90	523
FOX		44	9	53
Total		1,304	292	1,596
All characters	N	22,611	8,341	30,952
Males	%	68.2	74.3	69.8
Females	%	31.5	20.3	28.5
Indeterminate	%	0.3	5.4	1.7
Major characters	N	4,068	2,426	6,494
Males	%	66.9	79.6	71.7
Females	%	32.9	16.3	26.7
Indeterminate	%	0.2	4.1	1.7

This chapter focuses on comparisons of gender and age, both in general demographic and in some specific dramatic roles. It addresses these questions: How are characters of different ages and genders represented on television? What are the associations of these portrayals with different class, race, health, and other dramatic roles? What are the potential lessons of the television experience for growing up male or female and for aging as a social role?

The Aggregate Analysis

Age on television is a resource defined by dramatic formulas of gender and role (see Table 2). Female roles are less than one third of the prime-time character population. Although their percentage increased from 27.6 to 36.1 in 20 years, the proportion of midlife and older women remained approximately 15% of female characters, about half of the true proportion of the 45-and-over U.S. female population.

As television characters age, their proportional representation declines. Women's share declines faster than men's. For every 10 midlife males, there are 23 young males. But for every 10 midlife females, there are 46 young females. In other words, females tend to be concentrated in the younger age groups and "age faster" than men. The gender imbalance is especially striking in midlife: For every midlife female, a viewer sees nearly four midlife males.

After age 65, representation declines even further. The 20-year average of both genders aged 65 and above is 2.2 percent of the dramatic television population, which is about one fifth of the comparable U.S. population.

The pattern for major characters (see Table 3) shows that leading parts for older characters, and especially for older women, are even more scarce.

Saturday morning children's programs, not tabulated here, further extend but do not alter the prime-time pattern. The proportion of children and adolescents is of course higher than in prime-time. The corresponding decrease in the proportion of adults reduces midlife female characters from 15.5% in primetime to 10.6% in Saturday morning children's programs. The imbalance is even greater for major characters. Older women in leading roles are virtually absent. The child viewer sees about nine times as many major midlife male characters as major midlife female characters.

Table 2

Trends in Prime Time: Ages and Genders of All Characters

		1973–78	1978–83	1983–88	1988–93	Totals 1973–93
Totals						
Male	%	72.4	69.0	67.9	64.9	68.5
Female	%	27.6	31.0	32.8	35.1	31.5
Age						
Under 18						
Male		6.3	8.1	7.0	11.4	8.1
Female		12.1	12.6	11.3	16.2	13.1
18–44						
Male		65.8	60.7	63.6	60.5	62.7
Female		69.0	69.1	72.4	66.0	69.2
45–64						
Male		25.9	29.2	27.6	25.2	27.1
Female		17.0	15.9	14.3	15.2	15.5
65 and over						
Male		2.0	2.0	1.9	2.9	2.2
Female		1.9	2.4	2.1	2.6	2.2

Note. Percents are of gender within age groups. For example, the first column "Under 18" should read "6.3 percent of all males and 12.1 percent of all females are under 18."

Romance and Marriage

Romance is rampant in prime time. It dominates the lives of young women. It prevails through midlife for men but not for women. CI data (not tabulated here) show that over one third of young males and two thirds of young females are involved in romance. In midlife, the roles change. One out of five midlife and older males encounter romance. However, a negligible number (less than 1%) of midlife and older women experience a romantic relationship.

Not surprisingly, marriage is a more defining circumstance for women than it is for men (see Table 4). Men's roles on television are

Table 3

Trends in Prime Time: Major Characters by Age and Gender, 1973–1993

		1973–78	1978–83	1983–88	1988–93	Totals 1973–93
Totals						
Male	%	71.3	66.0	64.3	65.0	66.9
Female	%	28.8	34.0	35.7	35.0	33.1
Age						
Under 18						
Male		6.3	7.5	7.9	14.6	8.4
Female		9.7	11.6	9.3	14.5	11.0
18–44						
Male		65.2	60.0	63.9	59.7	62.5
Female		71.9	72.1	73.3	72.0	72.4
45–64						
Male		26.9	30.6	25.8	22.7	27.0
Female		17.7	14.6	15.1	12.1	15.1
65 and over						
Male		1.6	1.8	2.4	3.0	2.1
Female		.7	1.7	2.3	1.4	1.6

centered on a great variety of lifestyles to which marital status is not relevant. Therefore, more men than women in all age categories appear in roles whose marital status is indeterminate. Conversely, more women than men are characterized as married, twice as many for young and midlife women. However, older married men are more likely to play leading parts than older married women.

Class and Race

"Class" was determined by isolating "clearly upper"—obviously wealthy or high society—and "clearly lower"—visibly poor—from the large and indistinct "middle class." The class structure of gender and age is peculiar (see Table 5). A larger percentage of women than men are clearly "upper class" in each age group. The proportion of upscale

Table 4

Marital Status of Prime-Time Characters, 1973–1993

	All characters			Major characters		
	Male	Female	Totals	Male	Female	Totals
Age						
18–44						
Indeterminate	71.4	47.2	63.3	28.0	12.7	22.4
Not Married	20.7	35.9	25.8	55.7	63.9	58.7
Married	7.8	16.9	10.9	16.3	23.4	18.9
45–64						
Indeterminate	73.9	48.6	68.6	36.1	20.7	32.8
Not Married	11.8	20.2	13.5	33.6	40.8	35.1
Married	14.4	31.3	17.9	30.3	38.6	32.1
65 and over						
Indeterminate	58.3	45.9	54.3	23.1	10.5	19.7
Not Married	25.1	33.6	27.8	50.0	68.4	54.9
Married	16.6	20.5	17.9	26.9	21.1	25.4

women rises with age and importance of role. As midlife major characters, rich women are 16.3% of all midlife women, the highest of all age groups, compared with 13.0% of men. As older major characters, rich women are 10.5% compared to 1.9% of older men.

"Lower class" women, however, are less visible than lower class men. Poor older women are virtually absent from the world of television, despite the fact that in real life they outnumber poor older men.

Television has more roles for older African American females than for males, though none of them poor. Other racial minorities are virtually invisible at any age (see Table 6).

Health

Despite all the mayhem in prime time (most of it painless), injury and illness are rare (see Table 7). Only one of four major characters suffers from any kind of health problem, handicap, or disability.

Table 5

Socioeconomic Status of Characters, 1973–1993

	All characters			Major characters		
	Male	Female	Totals	Male	Female	Totals
Age						
18–44						
Clearly Upper	2.7	5.0	3.5	6.6	9.4	7.6
Middle	94.0	93.5	93.8	90.4	88.7	89.88
Clearly Lower	1.5	.6	1.1	2.1	1.4	1.8
45–64						
Clearly Upper	5.9	7.7	6.3	13.0	16.3	13.7
Middle	91.6	89.1	91.0	84.6	81.5	84.0
Clearly Lower	1.3	2.3	1.5	2.3	1.1	2.0
65 and over						
Clearly Upper	4.9	7.0	5.6	1.9	10.5	4.2
Middle	88.6	89.5	88.9	86.5	78.9	84.5
Clearly Lower	2.4		1.7	7.7		5.0

Infirmity generally rises with old age, but, unlike in life, older women are more likely to be shown disabled than men. While 26.3% of female characters aged 65 and over suffer from some disability, only 19.2% of the males do. How some of these configurations work out in the shows themselves will be shown later in the script analysis.

Fate

The moral force of popular fiction and drama is in its allocation of destiny. Unlike in life, television viewers learn the final outcome quickly and clearly. Who are the heroes and the villains, the victims and the victimizers? What is each group's calculus of risk as they grow old?

The answers to these questions are based on the 20-year totals of those characters whose depictions were reliably codable in terms of clear indicators of fate. For each set of indicators, two measures are used. The first is the percentage of characters within each gender and

Table 6

Race and Ethnicity of Characters, 1973–1993

Age	All Characters			Major Characters		
	Male %	Female %	Totals %	Male %	Female %	Totals %
Under 18						
White American	78.6	85.3	81.5	75.1	90.2	81.0
African American	18.9	13.4	16.5	21.2	8.2	16.1
Hispanic/Latino	1.6	.7	1.2	2.1		1.3
Asian/Pacific	.8	.5	.6	1.1	.8	1.0
Native American	.1	.2	.1	.5	.8	.6
18–44						
White American	83.7	86.9	84.9	87.7	92.0	89.3
African American	13.0	10.9	12.3	9.6	6.7	8.5
Hispanic/Latino	1.8	.8	1.4	1.8	.7	1.4
Asian/Pacific	1.1	1.2	1.1	.5	.5	.5
Native American	.3	.2	.3	.5	.1	.3
45–64						
White American	92.1	87.2	91.0	92.1	85.1	90.5
African American	6.1	11.2	7.2	7.1	14.3	8.7
Hispanic/Latino	.8	.7	.8	.7	.6	.6
Asian/Pacific	.8	.6	.8	.2		.1
Native American	.2	.3	.2			
65 and over						
White American	88.8	84.3	87.2	85.7	88.2	86.4
African American	9.2	15.7	11.4	10.2	11.8	10.6
Hispanic/Latino						
Asian/Pacific	.5		.3			
Native American	1.5		1.0	4.1		3.0

age group whose fate is presented in unambiguous terms. The second is the relative ratio obtained by dividing the number of positive by the number of negative indicators. The first measure shows the percents of different age and gender groups being cast in the different roles; the second measure, the relative ratio, indicates the "price" each group pays for being cast in a positive role.

Table 7

Injuries and Illnesses of Major Characters, 1973–1993

	Male %	Female %	Total %
PHYSICAL INJURY			
Under 18	10.7	2.6	7.5
18–44	7.0	5.2	6.3
45–64	7.9	5.7	7.4
65 and over	22.6	18.8	21.3
PHYSICAL ILLNESS			
Under 18	9.2	6.0	7.9
18–44	6.8	5.8	6.4
45–64	7.8	8.2	7.9
65 and over	17.3	15.8	16.9
MENTAL ILLNESS			
Under 18	1.9	2.2	2.1
18–44	4.1	3.5	3.9
45–64	2.4	1.1	2.1
65 and over		5.3	1.4
ANY DISABILITY			
Under 18	15.6	9.1	13.1
18–44	11.3	9.6	10.7
45–64	10.7	10.0	10.6
65 and over	19.2	26.3	21.1

Heroes and Villains

Older characters are as likely as younger characters to be cast in positive parts ("heroes"), but less likely to be cast as "villains" (see Table 8). Class and race make a difference in that the few older, lower class, and African American characters who are seen at all are the most likely to get positive roles. Villainy, on the other hand, is most likely to be young, upper class, male, and White.

When major roles are analyzed, however, aging tends to reduce chances of being "good" in both genders, and increase chances of being "bad" among men (see Table 9). The most likely to play evil roles are

Table 8

Heroes, Villains, and Ratios: All Characters, 1973–1993

	n total	% Heroes	% Villains	Ratio of villains to heroes (per 100)
MALE, 18–44	8,868	27.5	13.9	51
MALE, 45 & over	4,139	25.9	11.5	45
FEMALE, 18–44	4,489	31.3	4.5	14
FEMALE, 45 & over	1,153	31.3	5.6	18
SOCIO-ECONOMIC STATUS (1983–1993) MALE, 18–44				
Upper class	73	19.2	30.1	157
Middle class	2,566	23.4	12.4	53
Lower class	40	17.5	20.0	114
MALE, 45 & over				
Upper class	74	20.3	24.3	120
Middle class	1,164	22.3	9.8	44
Lower class	18	33.3	0.0	
FEMALE, 18–44				
Upper class	79	19.0	13.9	73
Middle class	1,481	22.9	4.3	19
Lower class	9	11.1	22.2	200
FEMALE, 45 & over				
Upper class	31	19.4	12.9	67
Middle class	363	22.3	4.7	21
Lower class	8	25.0	0.0	
RACE AND ETHNICITY (1978–1993) MALE, 18–44				
White American	4,648	24.0	13.7	57
African American	723	28.5	7.5	26
MALE, 45 & over				
White American	2,408	22.0	11.4	52
African American	166	30.1	4.8	16
FEMALE, 18–44				
White American	2,752	27.5	4.5	16
African American	345	26.1	3.5	13
FEMALE, 45 & over				
White American	680	26.6	5.0	19
African American	92	31.5	3.3	10

old, rich men (39% of that group), and upper class major female characters (19%). Being older and upper class also increases the relative ratio of villainy among major characters. As Table 9 shows, older and richer types pay a higher price than the others for being good.

Violence, Victimization, and the Risks of Life

Violence was also defined in a clear-cut unambiguously observable manner: hurting or killing or the threat of hurting or killing in any context. Each character involved in any violence was recorded as a perpetrator, victim, or both.

Whatever else violence is or does, it demonstrates power. In dramatic representation, involving about one out of five speaking parts and over half of all major characters, it is the cheapest and quickest way of showing who can get away with what against whom. Content analyses of prime-time TV have shown that there are about 5 to 6 violent acts per hour and 20 to 25 violent actions per hour on Saturday morning children's programs (Gerbner & Signorielli, 1990).

In general, young males commit and suffer most of the violence, with perpetrators and victims in fairly even balance (see Table 10). Although aging for women and persons of color reduces the chances of involvement in violence, it increases its risks. For every 100 young male perpetrators of violence, there are 112 victims. The comparable relative victimization ratios are midlife and older males, and midlife and older females, 125:140; midlife and older African American females, and midlife and older and richer females, 160:200.

Major characters experience more violence and also are more often injured (see Table 11). Therefore, their relative victimization ratios are lower. Their "pecking order" of relative victimization (the number of victims for every 100 major characters committing violence): midlife and older males, and midlife and older females, 96:111; midlife and older African American females, and midlife and older upper class females, 167:175.

Lethal violence involves 5.5% of all and 10% of major characters (see Table 12). Aging again cuts the likelihood of killing and increases risk of being killed—but only for women. The relative ratios of characters killed for every 100 killers are for young men, 124; midlife and older men, 120; young women, 146; midlife and older women, 160.

Major characters kill more, but are relatively less likely to get killed, unless they are older women. Their relative ratios of characters killed for every 100 killers are young men, 52; midlife and older men, 43; young

Table 9

Heroes and Villains: Major Characters, 1973–1993

	n Total	% Heroes	Villains	% Villains per 100 heroes
MALE, 18–44	1,538	57.0	13.6	24
MALE, 45 & over	716	46.9	17.0	36
FEMALE, 18–44	882	58.4	7.1	12
FEMALE, 45 & over	203	47.3	7.4	16
SOCIO-ECONOMIC STATUS MALE, 18–44				
Upper class	102	40.2	29.4	73
Middle class	1,390	58.3	12.4	21
Lower class	32	53.1	12.5	24
MALE, 45 & over				
Upper class	87	28.7	39.1	136
Middle class	607	49.6	14.2	29
Lower class	19	52.6	5.3	10
FEMALE, 18–44				
Upper class	83	33.7	19.3	57
Middle class	782	61.5	5.9	10
Lower class	12	16.7	8.3	50
FEMALE, 45 & over				
Upper class	32	28.1	18.8	67
Middle class	165	52.7	4.2	8
Lower class	2	0.0	0.0	
RACE AND ETHNICITY MALE, 18–44				
White American	1,275	57.2	13.7	24
African American	139	56.1	10.1	18
MALE, 45 & over				
White American	601	47.4	16.6	35
African American	48	50.0	2.1	4
FEMALE, 18–44				
White American	773	57.2	7.4	13
African American	56	62.5	5.4	9
FEMALE, 45 & over				
White American	164	48.2	6.1	13
African American	27	48.1	7.4	15

Table 10

Violent Perpetrators and Victims: All Characters, 1973–1993

	Total	% Involved	% Perpetrators	% Victims	Victims per 100 Violent Perpetrators
TOTAL (1973–1993)					
MALE, 18–44	8,868	34.5	24.8	27.7	112
MALE, 45 & over	4,139	23.2	14.6	18.3	125
FEMALE, 18–44	4,489	19.4	10.3	15.6	151
FEMALE, 45 & over	1,153	13.4	6.8	9.5	140
SOCIO-ECONOMIC STATUS (1983–1993)					
MALE, 18–44					
Upper class	73	46.6	34.2	32.9	96
Middle class	2,566	32.3	22.4	25.3	113
Lower class	40	45.0	25.0	37.5	150
MALE, 45 & over					
Upper class	74	25.7	21.6	17.6	81
Middle class	1,164	19.1	12.1	13.7	113
Lower class	18	27.8	5.6	27.8	500
FEMALE, 18–44					
Upper class	79	25.3	17.7	17.7	100
Middle class	1,481	15.3	8.2	11.5	139
Lower class	9	22.2	11.1	22.2	200
FEMALE, 45 & over					
Upper class	31	16.1	6.5	12.9	200
Middle class	363	12.4	6.3	7.7	122
Lower class	8	12.5	12.5	12.5	100
RACE AND ETHNICITY (1978–1993)					
MALE, 18–44					
White American	4,648	33.6	24.2	27.0	112
African American	723	30.4	20.1	23.2	116
MALE, 45 & over					
White American	2,408	20.9	13.1	16.2	124
African American	166	16.9	12.7	12.0	95
FEMALE, 18–44					
White American	2,752	18.9	10.3	15.0	146
African American	345	13.0	7.2	9.3	128
FEMALE, 45 & over					
White American	680	11.0	5.4	6.9	127
African American	92	10.9	5.4	8.7	160

Table 11

Violent Perpetrators and Victims: Major Characters, 1973–1993

	N	Involved	Perps	Victims	Victims per 100 Violent Perpetrators
MALE 18–44	1,538	63.7	51.6	54.4	106
MALE, 45 & over	716	46.8	37.0	36.5	98
FEMALE, 18–44	882	44.6	30.8	35.3	114
FEMALE, 45 & over	203	30.5	18.7	20.7	111
SOCIO-ECONOMIC STATUS					
MALE 18–44					
Upper class	102	53.9	46.1	45.1	98
Middle class	1,390	64.2	51.9	54.7	105
Lower class	32	68.8	53.1	68.8	129
MALE, 45 & over					
Upper class	87	50.6	44.8	40.2	90
Middle class	607	45.8	35.7	35.4	99
Lower class	19	57.9	36.8	52.6	143
FEMALE, 18–44					
Upper class	83	43.4	26.5	34.9	132
Middle class	782	44.8	31.1	35.4	114
Lower class	12	25.0	25.0	16.7	67
FEMALE, 45 & over					
Upper class	32	31.3	12.5	21.9	175
Middle class	165	28.5	18.2	18.2	100
Lower class	2	50.0	0.0	50.0	
RACE AND ETHNICITY					
MALE, 18–44					
White American	1,275	63.8	51.8	54.3	105
African American	139	100.0	43.2	46.8	108
MALE, 45 & over					
White American	601	45.3	35.6	35.3	99
African American	48	43.8	31.3	29.2	93
FEMALE, 18–44					
White American	773	44.4	30.7	35.2	115
African American	56	37.5	28.6	25.0	88
FEMALE, 45 & over					
White American	164	28.7	17.1	18.3	107
African American	27	25.9	11.1	18.5	167

women, 45; midlife and older women, 167. Killing by a major character with relative impunity is a male prerogative; they are often the enforcers of law and order. If and when older women get involved in violence, they are four times as likely to get killed as men of the same age.

As Table 12 indicates, at the bottom of the overall relative victimization "pecking order" are the relatively few older "upper class" female characters who get involved in violence, and the larger group of young black male characters, *all* of whom are involved in violence.

In general, then, women and characters of color pay the highest price for committing violence in the world of television drama. Young black males playing leading roles are more likely to be given roles in which violence may be justified, such as law enforcers, than are other young Black male characters. When rich women or young Black men in supporting roles commit violence, the retribution is fierce.

Personality Profile

Major characters in a special sample of prime-time programs whose casts included older characters were rated on several personality attribute scales. These scales include whether characters are treated with disrespect or pity, and whether they are portrayed as nuisances, stubborn, eccentric, or foolish.

More older characters are treated with disrespect than are characters in any other age group. About 70% of the older men and more than 80% of the older women are not held in high esteem or treated courteously, a very different pattern of treatment than that found for younger characters. Similarly, a much larger proportion of older characters than younger characters are portrayed as eccentric or foolish. A greater proportion of older women than older men—two thirds as compared with about one half—are presented as lacking common sense, acting silly, or being eccentric.

The script analysis that follows illustrates some features of the bird's-eye-view above, and contributes others that do not lend themselves to aggregate analysis.

The Script Analysis

A random sample of 50 scripts treating aging and older characters at some depth from 1980 through 1994 was examined to explore the plot

Table 12

Killers and Killed, Percent of All Characters, 1973–1993

	Total	Involved	Perps	Victims	Victims per 100 Killers
TOTAL (1973–1993)					
MALE, 18–44	8,868	7.7	3.9	4.8	124
MALE, 45 & over	4,139	5.9	2.9	3.5	120
FEMALE, 18–44	4,489	3.0	1.3	1.8	146
FEMALE, 45 & over	1,153	2.3	0.9	1.4	160
SOCIO-ECONOMIC STATUS (1983–1993)					
MALE, 18–44					
Upper class	73	17.8	6.8	12.3	180
Middle class	2,566	7.7	4.4	4.1	94
Lower class	40	12.5	7.5	7.5	100
MALE, 45 & over					
Upper class	74	9.5	5.4	5.4	100
Middle class	1,164	5.0	2.1	3.1	150
Lower class	18	16.7	0.0	16.7	
FEMALE, 18–44					
Upper class	79	7.6	7.6	0.0	
Middle class	1,481	1.8	0.8	1.1	133
Lower class	9	0.0	0.0	0.0	
FEMALE, 45 & over					
Upper class	31	3.2	0.0	3.2	
Middle class	363	1.1	0.3	0.8	300
Lower class	8	0.0	0.0	0.0	
RACE AND ETHNICITY (1978–1993)					
MALE, 18–44					
White American	4,648	6.0	3.4	3.3	98
African American	723	6.2	2.2	4.1	188
MALE, 45 & over					
White American	2,408	4.9	2.3	2.8	122
African American	166	1.2	1.2	0.0	
FEMALE, 18–44					
White American	2,752	2.2	1.1	1.2	113
African American	345	1.7	0.9	0.9	100
FEMALE, 45 & over					
White American	680	0.9	0.6	0.3	50
African American	92	1.1	0.0	1.1	

formulas, characterizations, and dialogues used to convey certain troubling aspects of gender and age on television.

Abandonment and Betrayal

Abandonment, betrayal, and even abuse by family, friends, and supposedly well-intentioned members of the community form the background to the aggregate findings of isolation from family context, infirmity, and mental illness. Of major women elders in the scripts studied, 63% were betrayed or abandoned by their families or friends while 42.8% of the major older males found themselves in a similar predicament. These elders were involved in plotlines that emphasized either that they preferred to be isolated or that they stubbornly acted in ways that prompted well-meaning family and friends to abandon them.

An episode of "Thirtysomething" exemplified this plot formula when it portrayed a clash of three generations: 80-year-old Rose Pollack, Rose's daughter Elaine in her 50s, and Elaine's daughter Melissa in her 30s. Elaine is portrayed as a dutiful and concerned daughter plagued by her mother's stubbornness and resistance to common sense. Rose is a woman with arrhythmia and congestive heart failure, but she resists Elaine's attempt to take care of her, and finds an ally in granddaughter Melissa.

Rose's increasingly controlling and irrational behavior finally alerts Melissa to the fact Elaine is correct after all: Rose is just a power-hungry, sick old woman, "an old bat on a throne." Melissa and Elaine decide to remove themselves from Rose's life and intervene only if "something happens to her." The last words of the script are a camera direction that makes clear that Rose is now isolated from the family:

> We move away from [Melissa] past a shelf on which all that remains are two
> framed photos. Rose alone, and Melissa and Elaine together.

Older male characters similarly struggle to maintain control, confront limitations attributed to age, and find themselves subdued or abandoned by children. However, male characters usually see the light by the conclusion of the episode and, unlike Rose, manage to salvage the reverence of younger family members.

For example, an older male character is portrayed in the "Wonder Years" in a situation similar to Rose's. "Gramps Arnold" loses his license after numerous accidents, but objects to his son Jack "telling him what to do" by keeping him out of the driver's seat. Like Rose, Gramps commandeers his grandchild Kevin as an ally, but unlike Rose, Gramps has enough logic to know when he is beaten and at the last moment earns Kevin's admiration by giving away his car. Gramps demands that Kevin drive away and leave him alone in the final scene.

When older parents spar with their adult children in the television world, it is best if the elders lose. If the older parents win as Rose did and succeed in pushing the children away, they will be abandoned. If the children win the battle and the elder complies with youthful authority, he or she gains respect. Yet ultimately, even the elder who submits to the authority of the younger generation ends up in isolation.

Older "winners" tend to be like the dying Mrs. Wilbourne from an episode of "A Year in the Life" who also refuses to take medication or obey other orders. Eventually she triumphs over her daughter Alice, refusing Alice's offer to move in with her and insisting that Alice leave her alone. "I said I never wanted to be a burden to my children. I raised you, don't own you," insists Mrs. Wilbourne. Alice drives off, leaving her mother to die alone.

Older "losers" who accept subordination by their children are usually men like Gramps. There is also Dominic Santini, an older fighter pilot in an episode of "Airwolf" who insists on undertaking a dangerous mission that he is no longer physically capable of executing. Dominic's former student, Hawke, fears for Dominic's safety and undertakes the mission himself. Dominic is not pleased with this betrayal and arguments and fistfights occur between the two of them. Eventually Dominic ends up in the back of the aircraft while Hawke successfully pilots them through the violent and dangerous mission. When the violence ends and the coast is clear, the shaken Dominic has come to his senses about his limitations, and Hawke is sympathetic.

> Hawke: If you'd like to take the controls I could use the rest.
>   (Dominic reacts)
> Dominic: I like it back here, just fine. (Hawke smiles)

Dominic accepts the fact his friend betrayed him "for his own good."

Burdens of Victimization

While benevolent younger people frequently subordinate older characters, predatory younger people also prowl the television landscape to rob or victimize (often) wealthy older women. For example, Margaret

Chase is a character whose victimization includes both overmedication and financial plunder. She befriends an evil younger man, Dutton, who renders her passive with medication and proceeds to steal her assets. Dutton succeeds until Margaret is rescued by a former lover. The rescue is tinged with tragedy; she soon dies of a terminal illness.

Violence is television's most obvious means of structuring power relationships. Violence against elders is usually depicted as a particularly evil kind of crime that is nonetheless a commonplace and largely unavoidable fact of life (Gerbner & Gross, 1976; Gerbner & Signorielli, 1990). An example occurs in an episode of "Beauty and the Beast", set in an apartment building in New York City. The script specifies that the building's tenants are all elders, and in addition there are strong hints that they are Jewish, with numerous Yiddish phrases used and particular foods such as *latkes* mentioned.

The anonymous building owner hires a management company to persuade the tenants to move out of the building. The script directs that Leo Mundy, head of the management company, is "a man past his prime, going soft in all the wrong places." Mundy and his gang conduct a crime spree against the tenants in an effort to scare them into leaving. One tenant, Micha Langer, is nearly killed by a fire bomb. Later when he and his wife, Sophie, are returning from the store, they are mugged. Two older female tenants report being robbed. One older man, Herman, relents and agrees to relocate, "his face swollen and bruised; he's been badly beaten."

The tenants are depicted as too terrified to emerge from the building, night or day. The plot reinforces older characters' statements that their suffering is deplorable but normal for the modern metropolis. Despite repeated incidents of terror and building code violations, neither the police nor the district attorney investigates the elders' victimization, claiming they are too swamped with other more pressing cases.

One day when Mundy's bullies invade the building, the assistant district attorney, Cathy, reluctantly convinced by a friend to investigate the situation, happens to be visiting the Langers.

> *The residents cower as the rooms are searched . . . . It's a night of terror. The sounds of thugs kicking in doors above is clearly audible, jarring the people's memory of another time, another place . . . .*

The script exploits images of the Holocaust to find a scene worthy of the level of violence and terror they seek to depict against elders. In the end, Vincent, the beast, comes to the rescue, single-handedly conquers the villains, and kills Leo Mundy. The viewer is left with the message that the level of criminal violence suffered by older people is akin to Nazi persecution of Jews, older people are incapable of defending themselves, and law enforcement couldn't care less.

Murdered Women

Among the major older characters in the scripts, three women and no men were victims of murder. Two of the women were the only two African American females.

The two African American women are depicted as kind and moral, savagely killed by fellow African Americans. One of the women is Bessie Copeland, a religious and disabled elder. After her nephew threatens her, she attempts to contact private detectives, but in the middle of the phone conversation the nephew strangles her to death. The other African American victim is Miss Kendrick, a music teacher who shows a special affinity for one particular African American student whom she nurtures through his childhood. That same teenager stands by and watches while his friends, other African American males, murder Kendrick.

The one White murder victim is Veronica Kirk, an aging movie star. Her daughter conspires to make her appear mentally ill, her colleague tries to rob her, and her best male friend murders her.

All three older women are major characters killed by the treachery of members of their family or close circle of confidants. By contrast, four men who are murdered are all minor characters whose murder results from business associations gone sour.

Mental Incapacity and Physical Decay

When private investigator Rick Simon arrives at the scene of Bessie Copeland's murder, the script directive explains what he finds there:

> *Bessie Copeland's wheelchair lies on its side at the foot of the stairs. A few uni-formed cops are huddled in casual conversation, showing no particular interest or concern . . . .*

Rick's statement that he heard Bessie being murdered over the phone fails to generate any alarm: "Maybe she got attacked by a pink elephant," the chief detective jokes.

Older White women are also portrayed as useless, although they manage to garner more sympathy than poor Bessie. In an episode of "Designing Women," five women characters go for an Outward Bound-style wilderness learning experience. The younger women are

Charlene and Suzanne; the older women are Bernice, Evelyn, and Dorothy. Bernice is a character who appears in other "Designing Women" scripts as a slightly discombobulated elder whose friends are in nursing homes. With Evelyn and Dorothy temporarily away from the campsight, Bernice has some choice remarks to make about them:

Charlene: Evelyn and Dorothy are sweet, aren't they? They remind
            me of those sisters who used to be on the Waltons.
Bernice: Yes, Charlene, they are sweet. But they're also old. I hate
            it, but if they can't keep up with the group, we'll have to
            dump 'em.
Charlene: Bernice, that's so cruel. Anyway, we're supposed to help
            each other.
Bernice: I know. But I looked in the manual and you get more
            points for leadership than helpfulness. And any good
            leader knows one of the first things you do is streamline
            the organization. Eliminate the dead weight.
Charlene: Bernice, I've never seen you this way. You're so incisive
            and energetic!
Bernice: I know! It's this wilderness air. My fog has lifted. I'm com-
            pletely invigorated.
Charlene: Well, that's great, but let's not get too carried away.
Suzanne: Don't discourage her, Charlene. At least she isn't saying
            something dumb. I think it's kinda nice to see Bernice on
            top of things.

According to formula, the writers used an older woman character to deliver this stark message, and Bernice is duly rewarded for it: At a ceremony on the final day of the leadership experience, Bernice is given an award for exhibiting the "highest standards of leadership."

Older women characters often note but do not address the fact that they are irrelevant in the television world. "My life ain't much but it's all I have," says Veronica Kirk, and the viewer cannot help but agree since she has not emerged from her house for the past 30 years. In an episode of "We Got It Made," Alice complains to her younger adult education classmates that "I don't have much charisma. When I'm on the subway, people sit on me."

With the exception of a few men portrayed as powerful, if aged, captains of industry, older characters are depicted as confused or muddled. Mental illness and growing intellectual incapacity are omnipresent symptoms of the aging process on television. Reference to mental conditions ranged from younger characters expressing worry about the growing confusion of parents to an elder announcing that her dog is actually her deceased husband, to references to a confused elderly mailman who delivers the wrong letters, to the disturbed elder on a homicidal rampage.

Sickness is seen as an inevitable and constant state of affairs of the older character. Older characters have no social or political clout, with older women the most subordinated and older African American women only pathetic victims. In contrast to the political strength of seniors in the real world, elders in the television world submit voluntarily to discrimination or are ridiculed, degraded, dismissed, and brutalized.

Ridicule

The majority of older women in the scripts are ridiculed, while only 20 percent of the men endure such treatment. Elders are most often ridiculed for supposed age-related traits. For example, in an episode of "Thirtysomething", Melissa and her grandmother Rose, mentioned earlier as initially close but later separated by Rose's controlling behavior, are in Rose's dressing room,

> Rose: *(looks in mirror)*
>   How's my makeup?
> Melissa: You look okay, for an old bag.
> Rose: *(Sits down)*
>   Thanks . . . where's my needlepoint?

This is meant to demonstrate equality and closeness between the two women, swapping a joke across generations. Yet, it is the older woman who must bear the burden of the joke. Rose's insecurity about her appearance is clear throughout the episode, yet she must tolerate biting ridicule in order to be granted an equal relationship.

Characters are often chided for supposed age-related mental infirmities. Middle-aged teacher Mrs. Russell is shown in an episode of "Head of the Class" with symptoms of Alzheimer's disease, and is eventually forced to resign. She later sends a postcard which one of the teachers, Charlie, reads to her class in the final scene. The script reads:

> Charlie: "Just hit London. Having a wonderful time . . . as far as I can
>   remember . . . . only kidding . . . . Hope all of you are well.
>   Miss you very much. Love, Queen Elizabeth.

(Class laughs, we cry, stay tuned for "Hooperman")

Older women's sex life usually involves unsuccessfully clamoring for a husband. However, in "The Golden Girls," two female characters are depicted as romantically involved (no other such midlife or older women turned up in the 20-year sample), prompting considerable witticisms that have an adolescent cruelty.

The dominant characterization of older women's sexuality, however, is the man-hungry, frustrated, wealthy widow. A group of them tour the White House and flirt with a younger man, which provokes great amusement. In an episode of "A Year in the Life," middle aged widower Joe inadvertently finds himself hosting a garden club meeting that consists entirely of widows. Joe's son jokes to his father, "You should see the way they look at you, like you're a hamburger and they haven't eaten in about a year."

Older women clamor for older men, but if older men do any clamoring, it is for younger women. Older men flirting with youthful women is depicted as "sweet." But a hint of sexual congress between an older woman and a younger man is seen as pathetic.

"The Golden Girls" Characters

Four older women and no man in the cast of "The Golden Girls" stands in sharp contrast with the demography of the television world. But, instead of departing from stereotypes in other respects as well, "The Golden Girls" follows the television formula for depicting older women, and in some cases exceeds it in bias and mean-spiritedness.

Like most of prime time's older women, all but one of "The Golden Girls" are widowed and roommates because they were isolated or abandoned by family and friends. Sophia's daughter Dorothy tried to put her in a nursing home, Dorothy's husband divorced her for a younger woman, and widows Rose and Blanche found themselves alone and financially at risk.

Within the "Golden Girls" universe, Sophia is the stereotypical old woman. She suffers a stroke, appears confused on occasion, is retired, and seems to have a limited lifestyle. She is insulted with age-related epithets and made to appear distracted and superficial. At her daughter's wedding, while the others are shown thinking about future happiness for Dorothy, she is depicted as obsessed with her aching hamstring.

The characters show no remorse in attacking the weakest and most vulnerable aspects of each other's psyche. They insult, demean, and ridicule each other with impunity, rarely exchanging words of affection or respect. Blanche is ridiculed with locker room jokes about her promiscuity. Sophia suffers insults for presumed symptoms of her age and infirmities. "Boy, you play that stroke like a Stradivarius," snipes her daughter. Dorothy is teased for her asexuality and unattractiveness to men, and Rose for her stupidity and affinity for telling long, absurd stories of her past life.

Conclusion: The Lessons

When seen from a bird's-eye-view, the contours of otherwise familiar territory are striking for their consistency and stability. Age on television is a resource defined by dramatic formulas of gender and role. As characters age, their representation declines. Midlife and older women virtually vanish from the screen in major, positive, and powerful roles. They tend to be both underrepresented and overvictimized, isolated, infirm, often ridiculed, and if both rich and old also evil and marked for murder. A child growing up with American television will rarely if ever see a mature woman as leader.

What are the lessons viewers derive from television about gender, age and violence? Data from numerous large national surveys (Donnerstein, Slaby, & Eron, 1994; Gerbner, Gross, Signorielli, & Morgan, 1986) indicate that long-term regular exposure to television tends to make an independent contribution to the feeling of living in a mean and gloomy world (see Donnerstein & Smith's excellent review in this volume).

For example, heavy viewers are more likely than comparable groups of light viewers to overestimate one's chances of involvement in violence and express a greater sense of apprehension than do light viewers in the same groups. Viewers who see members of their own group as having a higher calculus of risk for violence than those of other groups develop a greater sense of mistrust, insecurity, and dependence—the marks of minority status (Gerbner, Gross, Signorielli, & Morgan, 1986).

Other survey findings show that heavy viewers are more likely than matched groups of light viewers to think that older people are not open-minded and adaptable, are not bright and alert, and are not good at getting things done. All of these relationships are stronger among younger respondents, those between the ages of 18 and 29.

We found similar patterns in studies of adolescents. When we asked about 600 sixth to ninth graders "At what age does a man become elderly or old?" and "At what age does a women become elderly or old?" light viewers gave the combined average age as 57 while heavy viewers felt that people become old at 51. Most of these adolescents believe women become old before men do.

We did not find watching television to be associated with any positive images of older people. Heavy viewers believe that the elderly are in worse shape both physically and financially than they used to be, are not active sexually, are closed-minded, and are not good at getting things done. At the same time, television is telling young people that old age, especially for women, begins relatively early in life.

Even with the proliferation of channels on cable and satellite TV and the increasingly demographically targeted marketing strategies, the largest and most heterogeneous audiences share in common a vision of aging that is anything but productive. It cultivates conceptions that trap the elderly in limited and demeaning roles. The overall television image resists rather than assists efforts to increase the scope of gender equity and productive aging (Gerbner, 1994).

These patterns compose the cultural environment into which children are born and in which we all learn the roles of growing old as women and men. That historic transformation shifts much of the battle for productive aging to the cultural frontier.

REFERENCES

Donnerstein, E., Slaby, R. G., & Eron, L. D. (1994). The mass media and youth aggression. In L. D. Eron, J. H. Gentry, & P. Schlegel (Eds.), *Reason to hope: A psychosocial perspective on violence and youth* (pp. 219–250). Washington, DC: American Psychological Association.

Gerbner, G. (1994). Learning productive aging as a social role: The lessons of television. In S. A. Bass, F. G. Caro, & Y. P. Chen (Eds.), *Achieving a productive aging society*. Westport, CT: Greenwood.

Gerbner, G., & Gross, L. (1976). Living with television: The violence profile. *Journal of Communication, 26*, 172–199.

Gerbner, G., Gross, L., Morgan, M., & Signorielli, N. (1994). Growing us with television: The cultivation perspective. In J. Bryant & D. Zillmann (Eds.), *Media effects* (pp. 17–41). Hillsdale, NJ: Erlbaum.

Gerbner, G., Gross, L., Signorielli, N., & Morgan, M. (1986). Living with television: The dynamics of the cultivation process. In J. Bryant & D. Zillmann (Eds.), *Perspectives on media effects* (pp. 17–40). Hillsdale, NJ: Erlbaum.

Gerbner, G., & Signorielli, N. (1990). Violence profile, 1967 through 1988–89: Enduring patterns. Unpublished manuscript, Annenberg School of Communication, University of Pennsylvania, Philadelphia.

4

MTV, Adolescence, and Madonna: A Discourse Analysis

E. Ann Kaplan

A s a humanist addressing a readership largely comprising psychologists, a few preliminary words on method are in order. Like
most humanists, I deal with data; but my data are images of human
behavior in cultural artifacts, such as books, film, and television, rather
than observation of human behavior in laboratory or real-world contexts. My data are also the artifacts themselves—how they are produced, their history, their institutional settings, their dissemination.
Humanists test ideas about images and cultural institutions in discussion and debate with other humanists. For us, signs of excellence and
validity lie in thorough library and textual research, consistency of argument, plausibility, common sense, and the logical coherence of ideas.

Clearly, both psychologists and humanists are concerned about the
interaction between a given text and those receiving it, but they go about
analyzing this relationship in different ways. Where psychologists want

to find out how specific behavior is influenced by images, humanists are concerned about how meaning is produced, about the meanings viewers construct out of images, and about the larger relationship of different viewers to popular culture. Humanists are concerned with the level of representations, both inside and outside of people's heads. "Data" consist of images found in popular culture, and humanists have to rely on theory (and themselves) for understanding the image-world inside anyone's head. For such purposes, discourse theory provides the most promising method to date.

Discourse analysis derives ultimately from Foucault (1972, 1977) and consists of (a) isolating certain prevailing organizations of language (using that term broadly to include visual signs) in the public sphere, (b) clarifying the gender and class basis inherent in the discourses, and (c) exploring the hierarchical and power assumptions within the discourses. Discourse theory also involves sensitivity to history—to how past cultural traditions, codes, genres, and technologies have prepared for (and may account for) what is constituted in the present. The method usefully provides a way of linking fictional constructs and the level of daily lived existence. It postulates that there is a link between the realm of the fictional (the imaginary) and that of lived existence. Discourse theory suggests that the two spheres cannot be so easily distinguished. So much of the "daily" is taken up with discourses in the sense of fantasies, whether it be working hard with the end of fulfilling some "status" fantasy in the future, or buying goods (especially clothes) in the hope that they will magically change one's body or personality, and bring a romantic fantasy to life right now. As popular-culture scholars have argued in relation to "soap operas" (see Brunsdon, 1983; Modleski, 1983) popular culture may actually help solve daily problems, so that it becomes difficult to distinguish fictional discourses from discourses people live within outside of cultural productions. I continue to differentiate discursive formations within MTV from those outside it, but all are ultimately *texts* of one kind or another.

Following are four distinct discourses in relation to MTV and adolescent address, with specific focus on the period of the late 1980s and early 1990s: (a) select public discourses about MTV videos and rock stars (on TV, in newspapers), with reference to their historical bases; (b) discourses within select MTV videos, especially power-relations among different figures in videos; (c) the discourse of adolescents (usually repressed in dominant discourse), including uses adolescents make of popular culture, and the historical relation of women to this culture; and (d) discourses about rock stars in teen-consumer culture. Madonna—from her early period through 1992—will be used as a representative example in all four discussions for the sake of coherence and efficiency.

Public Discourses About MTV and Rock Videos

MTV is a commercial proposition. It is a 24 hour, nonstop cable station beamed to cable customers across America whose average age is between 12 and 34 years (totaling at the present time around 40 million people, up nearly 20 million since I wrote my book on MTV in 1987). Indeed, I argued in *Rocking Around the Clock* (Kaplan, 1987) that MTV may be seen on one level as a nonstop advertisement for a whole series of things. MTV does extensive market research in deciding which videos to promulgate (with particular attention to race, gender, class, and ideological aspects). They ask, "What is it that teens watching MTV want to see?" They then gear their images to correspond to some desire on the part of teen viewers out there whom their market research has located.

Parents meanwhile accuse MTV of "shaping" their kids in destructive ways. In 1990, the Parents Media Resources Coalition was active in demanding labeling of records with lyrics they claimed were obscene. Jeannette Dixon, a Missouri Senator at the time, filed many suits against record companies. On TV she blamed one young person's suicide on then pervasive rock star Ozzy Osbourne's "Suicide Solution" record, and two others on a supposedly subliminal suicide message in Judas Priest videos. The 1990 court case (Rimer, 1990) about 2 Live Crew's obscenities in a night-club act, presumed to be morally harmful to adolescents, shows the extent to which the public, and its representatives, are willing to go. In this case, the band members were exonerated, in part as a result of Henry Louis Gates' compelling arguments about the Black traditions that 2 Live Crew drew upon, including ironic satire of the White culture that has long oppressed Blacks (Gates, 1990). More recently, and as a result of parents' demands, cable companies have developed technologies to block out channels, like MTV, that preclude children from watching.

It is this parental discourse that dominates in the public sphere. I have argued elsewhere (Kaplan, 1990a) that the vociferous parental groups decrying the impact of rock on youth basically rely on an outmoded notion of the image as per se dangerous that dates back to

Plato's exiling of both the painter and the poet from his utopian Republic because the images they create are, for Plato, but copies of copies (objects in the real world, which in turn copy the "essences" in heaven). Or, as Socrates' interlocutor confirms, "You're using the term 'representer' for someone who deals with things, which are, in fact, two generations away from reality" (Plato, 1993, p. 348). Socrates shortly shows his scorn of people who revere such "illusionists," and, out of their own "inability to evaluate knowledge, ignorance, and representation, to have been so thoroughly taken in as to believe in his omniscience" (p. 349). The notion of the image as dangerous was but a step away from this, and has been recently revived by Allan Bloom (1988) and Neil Postman (1985). There is no evidence, however, of the image's inherent danger; it depends on the constructs of the viewer. In Medieval times, the image was thought to be particularly dangerous for men (seducing them off the beaten track, Freedberg, 1989). Usually the feared seduction was via images of women, showing that sex, explicitly, was at issue. Meanwhile, since women *were* the image, they were not theorized as having any relation to the image.

The parental discourse, then, arises out of a very old view which resurfaced first in debates about TV violence (see Hoffman, 1984; Donnerstein & Smith in this volume), and was carried over into fears about MTV's impact on youth. But what about the images of teenagers on MTV itself? What power-relations are evident within videos? What role does gender play?

Discourses Within Select MTV Rock Videos

The following section briefly describes the five basic types of MTV videos that were relayed across the nonstop, 24 hour "flow" of images and outlined in Kaplan (1987). These types are still relevant today, except that rap videos must be added as a separate category.[1] Arguably, rap videos could be subdivided into five types similar to those distinguished for the channel as a whole.

---

[1] In the last few years, MTV may have changed even more than adolescent culture as a whole. The channel has become even more like a mini-version of the whole of TV programming and is no longer simply a music channel. There are regular nonmusical series, including "Beavis and Butthead, "Shut up

To begin with, a brief survey of the types reveals the dominance of *male* adolescent culture on the channel. Brown and Campbell's quantifying study of MTV (1986) showed that videos featuring White males took up 83% of the 24 hour flow; only 11% at that time had central figures who were female, and the figure was even lower for Blacks. More Blacks are certainly being featured on MTV in the mid-1990s partly because of the increased popularity of rap music and videos in these years, and the percentage of women bands is surely much higher as well. But neither of these developments necessarily means more pro-Black or pro-women videos are readily apparent. Black and female artists' videos often embody perspectives congruent with White patriarchal culture. And rap artists such as Queen Latifah are unfortunately still a rarity. A quick sampling of current MTV revealed that male artists still predominate on the channel in prime time, although, as I discuss later, female-centered videos have always been on MTV, even if less attended to.

The first three types of videos—"nihilist," "classical," and "postmodernist"—all feature largely male groups. "Nihilist" videos are mainly produced by "heavy metal" bands, also referred to as "headbangers" (e.g., Ozzy Osbourne, Motley Crue, Aerosmith, Billy Idol, Judas Priest, Twisted Sister). These White male videos parade the male body, appeal often to fantasies of violence, including violence toward women, and address young males' frustrations and disillusion with contemporary adult life. Usually the stars are clad in tight pants, wield their instruments like phallic weapons, and assault the viewers directly. As the nickname "headbanger" implies, however, there is a great deal of self-consciousness about the sexism and the violence; a main provocative object seems to be to violate so-called "straight" adult values and institutions, like marriage, career, and the family. The videos are often explicitly sexist, showing scantily clad women, who are mere decoration in the videos—playthings for the male artists. In Poison's 1991 video, "Unskinny Bop," for instance, the women on stage become mere drawings, emphasizing their usual status as figments of male imaginations. The fact that female audiences seem to adore the bands, and are

---

and laugh," and "Real World," a series about young adults in a London apartment. In addition, during various holidays, MTV goes on location to sunny vacation spots where college kids tend to go and televises their antics to the viewers back home. Only a few times during the MTV broadcast day do you find plain music videos featured. That type of programming has become the format of the VH1 network.

an excited part of the audience, perhaps reflects an old paradigm, in which the release of female desire is masochistically geared toward sadistic male objects. More on this topic will follow later in this paper.

"Classical" refers to narrative videos, again largely but not exclusively by White male groups. These videos deal explicitly with sexual themes, usually with male pursuit of the desired female as the object of the male gaze (similar to familiar constructs feminist critics found earlier in film). The "classical" label indicates that a conventional paradigm, in which the male is bearer of the gaze, the female the desired object of the gaze, is in play.

Some videos made from lyrics of male groups in the 1990s have begun to feature a seductive female—the female apparently owning her sexual desire, instead of being the object of some other's sexual desire. A good example of this is Billy Idol's "Cradle of Love" video. The video differs from others of its type that show women only as passive objects of male desire in that the focus is on the woman's desire. However, it is soon obvious that this is a *male* fantasy of female desire, very much as was the desire of *femme fatales* in 1940s American films noirs. The heroine's desire in the video is at first inspired by a male image (Billy Idol himself, no less), even if later, in relation to a computer "nerd," the heroine is the seducer. What is important for my conclusions is the narcissistic depiction of female desire in videos like this one. Female desire is not presented as really concerned with the male object, but as related to the woman's infatuation with her own body. It is as if she is viewing her body through a male gaze, rather than outwardly directing her desire.

From a feminist perspective, such female portrayals are problematic. Humanities theories of identification as well as psychological empirical studies of television's impact on adolescents (Lowrey, 1988; Baran 1974) suggest that young women might well model themselves on such images. Modeling of this kind would severely limit the goals an adolescent might set for herself precisely at a time in life when she is deciding upon such goals. Modeling on passive images might inhibit a young woman's orientation toward autonomy from males, and toward fulfillment in satisfying work, career, or social activism.

The "postmodernist" type of video is perhaps the most complicated to explain briefly in this context. The term has been much debated in humanistic contexts over the past decade (Kaplan, 1988). For our purposes here, the word refers to a kind of video in which self-reflexivity is paramount, where well-known cultural texts, artifacts, and constructs are played with in a sophisticated, often elaborate manner. Jameson (1984/1988) and others have talked about the postmodern as replacing modernist parody with "pastiche"—a position that is not explicitly critical, that does not declare a position at all, and that is linked to contemporary forms of multi-corporate capitalists. Other definitions have a more positive association and are linked to the freedom from oppressive binarisms such as male/female, Black/White, high/low culture, and so forth. In this sense, postmodernism makes possible new roles, new subject-positions for hitherto marginalized groups, such as women, Blacks, and other ethnic minorities.

Male groups have tended to produce most of these videos as well. Often they are among the most aesthetically brilliant, and complex of videos (Kaplan, 1987). The videos clearly address sophisticated, educated, and articulate young adults. They often include sexist images, but the self-consciousness about such stances and the play with the construct of "sexism" puts them in a different category from the classical and nihilist objectification of the female body.

The remaining two types of videos are the "romantic" and the "socially conscious" videos. Many male bands make videos in both these categories, but I was particularly surprised to find how many romantic videos male bands made. In Kaplan (1987, pp. 98–101), I focus particularly on a haunting Paul Young video, "Every Time You Go Away," that seemed to me about preoedipal loss of the loved mother object. My study of the channel also showed that the socially conscious videos are mainly by male bands, and are the group least talked about in public discourses about MTV. Bands from the United States such as Bruce Springsteen, John Cougar Mellencamp, and Jackson Brown, as well as Midnight Oil (Australia), The Kinks, and other European groups, have made excellent and significant videos about pressing social issues from starvion in Ethiopia, war and poverty, and the plight of the farmers, to environmental disasters, nuclear holocaust, and apartheid (Kaplan, 1987, pp. 64–80).

Female Videos

The dominance on MTV of male adolescent culture, of male images of females, and their fantasies of female desire, evident in much of what has been highlighted so far, hides what else is going on: the roles of female stars and bands. Although less celebrated and less frequently

shown on MTV, many female stars have also made significant contributions in the "socially conscious" and "romantic" categories. However,
before referring to some specific videos, especially some featuring the
early Madonna, I will focus on the issue of women in popular culture.
This will in turn prepare for discussion of the third discourse, namely
that of female adolescents usually repressed in dominant discourse.

The topic of women and current popular culture is too vast to deal
with in any depth here, but one of the ways humanities methods differ
from those in psychology is precisely in turning to the historical perspective as essential for understanding the present. Phenomena relating to female adolescents and MTV may be usefully illuminated
through reference to the history of popular culture and to the history of
traditional male and female socialization, patterns that remain in the
present.

Historically, the impetus for popular culture was the existence of a
female audience for it. Men always had places in the public sphere that
they could go to for their pleasures (comradeship in the pubs and bars;
sports of all kinds on the street or in clubs or illegal spaces, such as
those where cock fighting went on; sex in brothels or with prostitutes
from the street). Until well into the twentieth century, however, women
had been confined to the family and the home until marriage, when
they were again confined. The novel developed into a genre for and by
women to give the bored middle-class housewife something to do at
home. Qualifying Ian Watt's (1957) theories, Terry Lovell (1987) and
Dale Spender (1986) have shown that the majority of eighteenth century novels were written by women. Novels were consumed by women
who, although busy with daily chores, were constrained by the limits of
the middle-class home. Novels were at once a convenient kind of pleasure (they could easily be picked up and put down) and opened up a
space for fantasies of experiences women had no access to at the time.
And so a need for popular culture, in the sense of mass imaginary
entertainment that satisfied desires and fantasies that real life could not
satisfy, was born.

But males quickly dominated this culture as well once the machines
for aural and visual pleasure (radio, photography, film, video) were
developed. Genres specifically geared to women were created, for
example the soap opera, which continued the melodrama, and the sentimental novel. In all these forms, women have a special closeness to
the image, in the sense of needing or wanting identification with figures like themselves. Scholars have argued that women exist in a rela-

tional mode toward these narratives, getting satisfaction from seeing frustrations (to do with love, marriage, family, the home) re-enacted (Mulvey, 1975, 1989; Doane, 1981). Men traditionally occupy a more distanced relationship in that they look at, and desire, women. Men are continually presented in terms of the public sphere—war, the State, crime, and the corporate world.

Historically, the sentimental novel and the melodrama showed female desire as the desire to win the romantic hero. Often, desire was enacted in a sadistic manner, such as women being forced into sex by handsome, commanding, rich gentlemen; or women being rescued by the hero from certain loss of virginity. Such images provided masochistic pleasure for the female reader.

In our own period, rock videos attest to totally new, and exciting, possibilities for young women to have access to cultural pleasures and cultural spaces outside the home, hitherto denied them. These are the pleasures of the visual sphere, of identification with desiring female *subjects*, and of public spaces like the shopping mall, as some critics have argued (McRobbie, 1980; McRobbie & Nava, 1984). Many rock videos show female subjects in the desiring position, pursuing their desired male objects, or simply enjoying their highly sexualized bodies (see Lewis, 1990; Roberts, 1996). I have divided videos featuring female adolescents into discrete types, most of which can, in turn, be fitted into either the "romantic" or the "socially conscious" categories. But some of the most satisfying videos belong in a special category, the playful video, which simply shows women having fun together. Cyndi Lauper initiated the "playful" video with her aptly named "Girls Just Want To Have Fun," but Bananarama, the Bangles, and others have continued it. Women in these videos enjoy each other, unconcerned about males. The videos have a light, tuneful quality, and foreground female bonding or females working or playing together in nonsexual ways. The Bangles' "Summer" actually shows the women repairing and washing cars together, violating a traditional concept that cars are only for males.

Many of the female videos made between 1984 and 1986 fall into the "socially conscious" type (Kaplan, 1987). Videos by stars like Tina Turner, Annie Lennox, and Pat Benatar in this period showed, first, special consciousness about women's plight in a patriarchal culture; and second, the desire to see women as autonomous and as fulfilling many, varied roles, not only those of wife, mother, or mistress. With Turner, there is the further interesting element of the use of female sexuality and female desirability to males, for the woman's own ends.

Tina Turner was historically important in opening up room for Black female rock music performers on MTV. Black women and men had traditionally been excluded from mainstream White dominated culture as many critics have now shown.[2] Black women singers had always had a place in jazz circuits and live performance, but primarily within metropolitan areas, playing to select audiences. Even in the late 1980s, Black women were still having a hard time being portrayed in other than stereotypical ways in Hollywood film and television (see Hooks, 1992; Wallace, 1990; and Kaplan, 1996). Thus, Tina Turner's inclusion on MTV in a top-ranking video, "What's Love Got To Do With It?" (1984) marked an important change and an opening for Black performers.

Turner's video was also important in initiating a stance more resistant to normative gender codes than many female rock videos are. (Indeed, I would argue that Madonna, who is said to have envied Black women in her Detroit High School, may have learned how to love her own body from her Black female peers, although I have not seen others make this argument.) Few MTV videos in the later 1990s take up really oppositional or resisting stances. If at first MTV offered some kind of rebellious or subversive space, the larger culture increasingly appropriates these spaces through advertising or mainstreaming so that the counter-cultural edge is eroded. To continue a subversive or resisting edge, women moved into the marginalized Punk and "Riot Grrrls . . ." spaces, where real difference from mainstream femininity could be developed and enjoyed.[3]

Other Black stars like Whitney Houston, Janet Jackson, and Paula Abdul quickly followed Turner's lead before largely Black male rap groups, many including women, became popular on MTV. But, as will be shown, rarely did these women exude Tina Turner's kind of resisting, challenging femininity. Other images of female desire, whether by

---

[2] The bibliography for research on images of African Americans in literature, arts, and the media is too extensive to list here. For a sampling of research and bibliography, see the pioneering collections of Henry Louis Gates, Jr. (1985) and Manthia Diawara (1991) that later developed into a book. See also Michele Wallace (1990).

[3] See, for example, Kim France (1993) and Debbie Goad (1993). See also materials produced by the group, Riot Grrrl NYC, who publish a magazine with their group's title. This information is culled from the in-progress research project of Theo Cateforis and Elena Humphreys, titled *Constructing Communities and Identities: Riot Grrrl New York City.* I am working at Stony Brook with graduate student Humphreys on this project.

Black or White artists of the late 1980s, were more traditional: Janet Jackson typified stars who present a sexual body, which is athletic, vital, but clearly still geared for a male gaze. Nevertheless, the presence of the female star's body at the center of the video and its narrative makes a significant difference from the male-centered "classical" type where the woman is a mere passive object of male desire.

But what about the discourses of teenagers themselves, outside of the videos, as receivers of the videos? This discourse is rarely given space in dominant media (being confined to specialized magazines—with the notable exception of the Sally Jesse Raphael show on "Madonna mania," which is discussed later in this chapter), and it is this (muted, repressed) discourse that I turn to now.

Repressed Discourses of Teenagers

Looking broadly, we can see that MTV, teenage spectators, and parents each occupy one point of a triangle. The teenagers are caught in the middle, growing up as they are in a period of particular stress and unprecedented responsibility. I have in mind here not only new sexual freedoms, with the responsibility for pregnancy and child rearing; not only AIDS, with all that entails in relation to responsibility; but also the most recent census showing that 50% of young people are living in one-parent homes, with the responsibility that, too, involves. Indeed, the tensions among the three groups arise precisely because hitherto generally unquestioned codes regarding gender, sex, race, and the family have come into question.

In the following discussion of some specific MTV videos, it will become clear that rock videos address some of these tensions. They perhaps help to release them in beneficial ways, and offer young females a new space where hitherto forbidden aspects of their lives, particularly in regard to sex, can be articulated. In fact, young females today have finally won the right to have pleasure in images, as part of the general loosening of females' cultural possibilities noted above. This new-won freedom coincides, not coincidentally, with the new freedom to be sexual and to accept one's own sexual desire. But the issue of new female sexuality is complex, contradictory, and contested. Different kinds of arguments are being made about it in cultural studies research, depending on the degree to which scholars emphasize positive aspects of "girl culture" and teenage consumerism, and the degree to which they view consumerism (and its impact on girl culture) negatively. The debate is essentially among those (a) arguing for "girl culture" as a distinct (and positive) culture in its own right (McRobbie & Nava, 1984; Lewis, 1990); (b) those concerned about young women's objectified position (Frith, 1981), and the commercial basis to the culture (Kaplan, 1987); and (c) those who stress that *processes of identification* are "normative" per se, leading as they do to "denial of one's identity, or to having one construct identity based on the model of the other . . . maintaining the illusion that one is actually inhabiting the body of the ego ideal" (Friedberg, 1990).

In what follows, the various merits of all three perspectives will be debated, using Madonna as a representative case study. Madonna brings together some main themes here, namely those of (a) female adolescent address in videos, (b) female adolescent needs for identification (in their search for *identity*), (c) recent changes in representations of female sexuality, and (d) the conceptualization of female consumption.

Particularly in the wake of her role as the parody of the 1940s femme fatale in the 1990 film *Dick Tracy*, Madonna was perhaps the one current rock star (outside of Michael Jackson, who has continued in that public spot) who captured the most public attention. The unprecedented 1992, 24 hour "Madonna-thon" on MTV attests to her status as icon of the pop-world, and to her enormous productivity. That there was enough Madonna "material" (videos, interviews, commentaries) to be circulated for so many hours (of course with repetitions) was itself extraordinary. Analysis of Madonna's spectacular (and calculated, hard-earned) rise to fame lies beyond my task here. But her fascination to particularly *female* fans is germane to my topic of MTV and adolescence. What was, and remains, Madonna's appeal to young women? What did they find in her manner, stance, and attitudes in the world of her videos that drew them?

An issue of a teen-magazine, *YM* (July 15, 1990) tells a bit about young fans' interest in Madonna, because fans sent in questions which the magazine then asked Madonna in an interview. According to the magazine's selection of questions to print, fans wanted to know what it is like to be famous, how Madonna felt about herself in school, what Madonna's love-life is like, how she keeps so fit, what music she likes and listens to—all of which presumably concern the teens asking the questions. My favorite interchange is when the *YM* reporter asks, "What kinds of cookies do you like to bake?" Her reply, "Next. I DON'T

BAKE," said with a vehemence indicating Madonna's deliberate refusal of the patriarchal feminine image of housewife-in-the-kitchen. There are two significant moments when Madonna is asked about the "Don't Bungle the Jungle" benefit for rain forests, and about what one element in her environment she would want to change. Madonna came out strongly for doing something about saving the forests and against "sexism, racism, bigotry, homophobia, and misogyny."

Equally important for my concerns here is how the magazine itself constituted Madonna as a particular kind of object, how it used teenagers' interest in Madonna to sell the issue and to reinforce teenagers' fascination with her to serve their own commercial ends. The magazine included in the same issue a questionnaire for teenagers to rate themselves in relation to Madonna. The questionnaire was headed "Are You A Material Girl?" referring of course to Madonna's famous video ("Material Girl"), which itself referred back to Marilyn Monroe, Madonna's own fan-object and "look-alike." The magazine, in addition, gave readers a quiz on Madonna-knowledge, the prize being a "Madonna Breathless-Dress." They were implicitly asking, "Do you identify so much with Madonna that you know all her likes and dislikes?" and stating, "If so, you have won the dress that will make you look like her as well." The whole magazine traded on the assumption that its readers do identify strongly with Madonna, do want to look like her, do model themselves on what is presumed to be her preferred "lifestyle." Significantly, there was no mention in the quiz of Madonna's political stances noted above.

I was reminded of this issue of *YM* magazine when I was invited to participate in a Sally Jesse Raphael show on "Madonna Mania." I was to be the "expert" for a program featuring mothers of daughters who were Madonna look-alikes and fervent Madonna fans. One mother-daughter pair was in conflict over the daughter's Madonna addiction, the other mother was more supportive of it. Between the back-and-forth debates were interludes in which night-club performers, who adopted Madonna personae and costumes, performed for the audience. As always, Sally Jesse interleaved panelists' debates with audience reactions and arguments. Both of the daughters were dressed as the *Dick Tracy* heroine, "Breathless," and shared some of the sentiments of the teenagers in *YM*. Before I go on, I would like to speculate a bit on what Madonna's attraction to adolescents might have been between 1986 and 1993.

Who's That Girl?

Madonna's first image (1983–84) was her bordello-queen, bag-lady image. She began her video career with a creative video, "Borderline," that already seemed to comment on woman's vulnerability to male desire, male fickleness, and male need to control woman's look. Already, Madonna's style was unique, outrageous, and daring. The attraction here may well be that of being different from Mom, and (for these teenagers) defining themselves that way.

It is important to have in mind that not all teenagers want to be different and that many teens are caught up in the desire to be the same as Mother, particularly in the desire for the patriarchal feminine of the establishment typified in *Cosmopolitan* and by popular models, and exemplified in such competitions as "Miss Teen USA" and the "mother-daughter pageants" that started in 1989. This teenager wants to belong to the middle-American norm, and she is the one much of rock culture developed to contradict in the first place.

Madonna's "bag lady" image was the furthest of all images from dominant feminine codes, and it was evident in several videos of this period. "Like a Virgin," for instance, both the video and the performance, deliberately violates and plays with "straight" cultural female images. It dares to link virgin and whore, in fact, to show the bride as the whore. "Dress You Up (in My Love)" and "Gambler" continued the image, but it came into its own with the film *Desperately Seeking Susan* (1985) and "Into the Groove," the video from the film soundtrack.

Teenage identification with this image of Madonna surely had to do with getting out of the patriarchal norm, while remaining sexy. Madonna talks often about how in school she was considered the "weirdo," the one different (King, 1991). She has even said that she envied Black girls' way of dressing, especially their hair, because they could be so different legitimately. The daring violation of specifically Catholic sexual norms, while still holding onto the cross, was particularly attractive to teenagers in this first stage of Madonna's image. It was the combination of the nun and the whore image—what a violation of codes. It was at this point that Madonna "look-alikes" proliferated—a phenomenon once again exploited by consumer entities. One example was Macy's Madonna look-alike clothes campaign that teenagers flocked to in order to actually be able to look like Madonna, the bag-lady, bordello queen, who nonetheless still claimed her religion in the cross that was such an important part of the get-up.

Madonna's "Material Girl," Marilyn Monroe image has been interpreted (Kaplan, 1987) as a postmodern video because of its ambiguous relation to Marilyn Monroe and its self-consciousness about the concept of the "material" girl. Certainly, the video plays with this ambiguity. Yet teen magazines seemed to take it quite seriously, and to ask teenagers to debate the degree to which, and in what ways, they were themselves "material." In that as in other videos, Madonna was most likely trying to have it both ways; that is, she wanted at once to critique a cultural phenomenon of excessive materialism (this was the hey-day of the "yuppies"), but at the same time not insist on a subversive position that might harm her popularity or the willingness of commercial institutions to sponsor her. I will return to this later in the chapter.

Madonna's constant image-change over the short space of 5 years is surely yet another attraction to young women, giving them a sense of the constant possibility for being *different*, for experimenting with different modes, styles, and fashions—for being someone else (the quotes cited later in this discussion from the Sally Jesse Raphael show on "Madonna Mania" fully bear this out). Madonna's main appeal, however, may be the image she projects of a sexy woman who, nevertheless, does not insist on being the object of a male gaze. Madonna often flirts with the camera, but the address is not at all necessarily, or exclusively, to males. She projects a sexiness that is in control of itself, that belongs to the heroine for her own use, and that suggests sometimes quite explicit lesbianism (as in her documentary, *Truth or Dare*, 1991). In this sense, some of Madonna's strategies are like those of Tina Turner, Annie Lennox, or Pat Benatar. Madonna's videos may provide young women with a healthy concept of what it means to be sexual and *not*, as in the male videos discussed earlier, simply the object of male desire, merely decoration behind males, or, as in the Billy Idol video, exercising seductive power over shy men. (Indeed, "Material Girl" may be read as precisely a friendly critique of this sort of woman: That is Madonna partly wants to be the "Monroe" woman, while at the same time wants to be far more autonomous than Monroe was able to be.)[4]

---

[4] By this I mean that Monroe was limited by her historical moment from access to the liberatory female discursive formations that Madonna came into as an adult. The simply seductive woman betrays her need of men, her need to have men desire her. She wants to be at man's behest, ultimately. Madonna, on the other hand, scorns such reliance on male desire. She prefers to retain control, even if this means turning men away by a parodic stance. Her sexuality is first for her own pleasure, only secondarily to make men desire her.

Several of Madonna's videos take up important social issues, even if these issues are not explicitly foregrounded or a particular position is not fully developed, as in some of the male socially conscious videos, or as in some of the female videos discussed earlier. "Papa Don't Preach" dealt with the issue of teenage pregnancy at a moment when cultural discourses were full of the problems of such pregnancies; "Open Your Heart" at once provided perhaps titillating images of a female porno-graphic performer for male viewers, but at the same time it portrayed such sexual arousal in the men in the porn parlor as rather ridiculous. The types of men portrayed probably fit many viewers of the video, perhaps eliciting some sort of self-reflection on the part of males. For women, there was perhaps pleasure also in seeing Madonna's body in the pornographic clothes, but obviously, Madonna's stance toward such dress was clear by the video's end, when she abandons it all together, as well as the porn house, to go off in her innocent, androgy-nous clothes, dressed like the little boy waiting for her all along.

"Like a Prayer" importantly overstepped several cultural taboos, that of sexuality and religion, that of Black and White intercourse, and that of Black and White relations generally. Madonna has been important in providing images of cross-ethnic relating, and for opening young peo-ple up to positive images of such relations. While the fantasized romance in a church with Madonna and the Black Jesus figure may have been sacrilegious to some, the bonding between the heroine and Black women and children in "Like a Prayer" was important in pointing out to young people that it is possible to overcome racial barriers that we know still predominate. Meanwhile, "Express Yourself" provides explicit instruction to women to look after themselves in sexual rela-tionships, not to settle for too little, and to ask male partners to express themselves and to give the woman pleasure (Kaplan, 1990b).

"Justify My Love," which appeared in 1992, joins together many of the concerns in Madonna videos over the past year. Incredibly stylized, the video extends the fascination with late expressionism already evi-dent in "Express Yourself" and the interest in the body and movement that "Vogue" epitomized. The aesthetic, stylized decadence of "Justify My Love" is reminiscent of many Fritz Lang movies of the late 1920s and early 1930s, especially *Metropolis* and the Dr. Mabuse series. Shot in black and white, the video's narrative is simple: An exhausted woman, returning from a voyage, recalls her lover and begins to masturbate in a hotel corridor. A stranger emerges from a room, begins to make love to her, and pulls her into an apartment where various groups of people are engaged in diverse kinds of love-making. Meanwhile, a lithe male figure, in black, dances around the lovers, his agile body swooping and swirling in ways reminiscent of the dancers in "Vogue."

The video is erotic in the manner of soft-pornography, but to mention the genre is simultaneously to highlight the contrast. The video's aim is not erotic arousal per se, but exploration of sexual desire, sexual need. The video's lyrics, similar to those in "Express Yourself," consist of an address to a lover: the heroine questions her lover about whether she is in his dreams, whether he fears her, and she confesses her need of him. Meanwhile, the camera moves restlessly over the figures, capturing faces made up to look like beautiful masks, and bodies mutually desirous. The solemn erotic mode is broken only once, when the camera catches Madonna's face, between two women making up each others' faces—and she offers the camera a self-conscious grin.

The video assumes a highly sophisticated, mature viewer. Its sexually explicit nature ensured that it would create even more controversy than earlier Madonna videos had done, and it demonstrates how Madonna has outgrown her "wannabee" 1986 fan base, now addressing a much older, urbane, postfeminist group, conscious of postmodernist strategies, and with some knowledge of art and film history. Audiences grow up with their rock star fetishes, it seems. According to some research (see Schulze, White, & Brown, 1993), many teenage women today no longer idolize Madonna.

MTV's censorship of "Justify My Love" made it an overnight *cause celebre*, and resulted in Madonna being interviewed on *Nightline* (December 3, 1990). Madonna put up a spirited defense of herself as an artist interested in expressing herself, whose aesthetic theme has long been a sexuality that degrades no one and that does not involve violence. She noted that parents do not complain so heavily about either sexism or degradation of women on MTV as they do about Madonna's open expression of sexuality, and argued for warning labels rather than censorship.

But what do teenagers themselves think about Madonna's carrying explicit sexual images to an extreme? I had a chance to find out something when I was invited onto Sally Jesse Raphael's talk show in 1993. This show featured Madonna in the wake of the publication of her now notorious book, simply called *SEX*. This was the period when Madonna was beginning to lose her teeny-bopper fans—those who had rallied to her bag-lady/bordello queen image that culminated in the popular role she played in *Desperately Seeking Susan* (1985) and that I discussed earlier on the chapter—and may have been concerned that her role as Breathless in *Dick Tracy* was not catching on as well. *SEX* followed hard upon the shock waves Madonna had just sent with her video "Justify My Love," which was not only sexually explicit, but depicted fantasies of orgiastic group sex with tinges of sado-masochism. *SEX* shows Madonna still trying to shock, of course, but reaching out to an older audience. It epitomizes her carrying to an extreme a concern to make *female* sexual fantasies as culturally permissible as *male* sexual fantasies have always been. But, predictably, Madonna's style was to do this in ways designed to provoke media and public attention.

What interested me about Sally Jesse's "Madonna Mania" show was, first, how alive Madonna fandom still was in 1993. Sally Jesse had gathered for the purposes of her show not only the mother-daughter pairs I had been told about, but also several Madonna groupies and some artists who made a living out of doing Madonna look-alike performances in New York clubs. These performers were most interested in Madonna's "bordello queen," "Open Your Heart" (sex-shop corset costumes), and Monroe images, while the young women on the show were dressed as Madonna "Breathless" look-alikes.

When asked why they dressed like Madonna and what attracted them to her, they gave these answers: "I did think I was Madonna at one time. I thought I was going to be a star, a super star . . .," and "I have loved Madonna forever, since I was five. I find Madonna attractive. She has an aura of mysteriousness. People are attracted to her and I like attention." When pressed by Sally Jesse to say what Madonna meant to them, one woman answered, "She has this energy about her . . . she's creative. She's created a vision. She idolized Marilyn Monroe. . . . Her image basically is power: power to do what she wants and she can do it. She (Madonna) says, 'I'm a star, and you're not.' If I was a star, I would feel the same."

Sally Jesse managed to get a debate going between two young women in the studio audience. One said, "For years, I dressed like Madonna. She had a great influence on me. I lived with her every day. I've grown up with her. It's how parents raise their children—that is how they are going to grow up." The other woman disagreed and argued against Madonna's open sexuality as "nothing to be proud of." This woman said she would be afraid to have children because of Madonna's influence, and that she was scared to sit on the couch and watch TV through fear of seeing someone with their legs spread.

Madonna showed "things you don't want to look at." The first woman argued that Madonna is a strong woman who "is showing women how to come out into the 1990s."

The 1993 Sally Jesse show debate indicated how controversial Madonna's exploits and images still were in the general public's mind. I objected to the way the show was biased against Madonna's efforts to show society's hypocrisy in regard to sexuality. When I tried to argue that society turned a blind eye to offensive male sexual fantasies, which proceed unimpeded in porn theaters and magazines everywhere, while berating Madonna for daring to "go public" with her own sexual fantasies, I was, in turn, upstaged by the president of Morality and the Media, who was given a long last word. My view that Madonna was dealing in sexual *fantasies*, not advocating "perverse" sexual practices, was only accepted by a few in the audience.

Conclusion

The analyses of select videos on MTV show that the channel is a complex, contradictory phenomenon, and that its content embodies a variety of adolescent fantasies, desires, and wish-fulfillments, as well as varying social values. The plethora of different adolescent-oriented material on the channel suggests an attempt to appeal to very different socially constructed groups in the United States today. Surely different groups of teenagers and young adults use the channel in varied ways, and also make use of Madonna (as it were) in different ways. Much empirical work needs to be done regarding differences in usage of MTV and Madonna on the part of teenagers from different ethnic, socioeconomic, educational, and gender groups. The internal discourses that teenagers bring with them will surely determine meanings they derive from the videos and from Madonna as rock star. While marketers make an effort to match up discourses within videos with those of specific social groups, obviously these matches are not perfect.[5]

For females (my particular concern in this chapter), popular culture is an ambivalent phenomenon. There are, as has been shown, some positive aspects of girl culture—the shopping malls, female bonding, the

---

[5] See *Newsweek*, August 1990 for a summary of some main teenage groups.

clothes, and the new possibilities that many videos offer for sexual arousal and healthy pleasure in sexy bodies of either gender. The kind of image the early Madonna offered of a sexy body, without the corresponding subjection to the male gaze, to male desire, is important. Madonna and other female rock stars make themselves subjects of their videos. They control the narrative, they express their desires, frustrations, grief, joys, and so forth, and this is positive for females identifying—as do the young women quoted above from the Sally Jesse "Madonna Mania" show—with the stars in terms of women gaining self-confidence, affirmation of sexuality, and affirmation of self-expression in a variety of ways. This self-expression includes creating outfits that are original and that differ from the patriarchal norms found in the "Mother-Daughter Pageants" or "Miss Teen USA" shows, which involve, in my opinion, more obnoxious commercialism than anything on MTV.

Other scholars, for example, Camille Paglia, have reduced the Madonna phenomenon to a simple utopian reading that ignores the complexity of her cultural images (Paglia, 1990). In her article, Paglia first reduced all the complex and multiple 1990s feminisms to one historically necessary, if now no longer needed, early 70s strand, which fought to protect women sexually and dared to reject dominant culture's stance on rape as woman's deep-seated desire. Paglia claimed that feminists "have been outrageously negative about Madonna from the start," ignoring the work noted above.[6]

Although Paglia repeated arguments similar to mine about Madonna's liberatory possibilities, she avoided the ensuing complex arguments about the contradictory nature of Madonna as a cultural object. Madonna clearly challenges conventional images while also, significantly, taking care not to step over a certain line which would harm her popularity, or would make her too marginal, physically or ideologically. Madonna has flirted with the underground avant-garde culture.

---

[6] Cf. Camille Paglia (1990). Here Paglia repeats what feminists like myself have already said about Madonna's positive impact on teenage women, while, in the same breath, lambasting feminists for their "puritanism and suffocating ideology." In a 1983 conference paper, later reworked for *Rocking Around the Clock*, I wrote that "It is perhaps Madonna's success in articulating a desire to be desired in an unabashed, aggressive, gutsy manner (as against the self-abnegating desire to lose oneself in the male that is evident in the classical Hollywood film) that attracts the hordes of 12-year old fans who idolize her and crowd her concerts" (p. 126). In my opinion, Paglia went too far in attacking feminists monolithically in the *New York Times* article.

She knows about it, and she still touches base with it at times, as in her interest in the gay and transvestite art forms called "voguing" (see her video "Justify My Love" and her public flirting with lesbian identity in shows with Sarah Bernhardt). In addition, Madonna participates in liberal causes, such as environmentalism and antiracism, as well as in more radical ones like antipatriotism or antiCatholicism. But she wants only to go so far, for fear of losing some segments of her audience. Commercial concerns, profit and the desire to keep huge numbers of fans, take precedence. Paglia praised Madonna's shrewd business talent (a talent that resulted in Madonna earning $39 million in 1990), but failed to see the inevitable exploitation of young women that may be involved. Consumerism depends on young women's unstable identities and their fantasies that, by buying Madonna "look-alike" clothes, they can be as rich, popular, and successful as Madonna. Although it is impossible to know what Madonna really thinks or whether she worries about her impact, some of her statements (as in the ABC *Nightline* interview with Forrest Sawyer in 1990) suggest she has a mission to combat sexual hypocrisy in mainstream U.S. culture, and to encourage women to be less personally and sexually dependent on men. But she shows little awareness of how the consumerist mechanisms she relies on may exploit adolescents' desires, fantasies, and psychic needs.

This is the era of the look, and the look-alike. Scholars need to take into account what it means for teens to model themselves on a star like Madonna, who is cannily aware of increasing her fame and fortune, while avoiding the mainstream feminine. The way that teen magazines encourage such modeling, as in the case of Madonna noted above, should be analyzed. Teen culture is an enormous market. The circular pattern mentioned at the beginning of this chapter clearly operates. In this pattern, teen fantasies, already the product of patriarchal socialization, are further reinforced by market research that decides what teens want and what will bring producers, like MTV, profit.

So although MTV female culture seems positively refreshing and full of vitality and excitement by contrast with mainstream femininity, too utopian a reading of it would mislead. It would suggest that teenagers are more in control of this culture than they may actually be. The stars like Dire Straits in "Money for Nothing," Talking Heads in "Burning Down the House," or the Kinks in "How Do I Get Close?" who comment on sexism, voyeurism, and commercialism are important. They indicate that MTV is willing to be self-reflective, as do program additions such as "Pirate MTV" and most recently, "Beavis and Butthead" cartoons.

However, every such example is balanced by something like the Billy Idol paradigm, which is narcissistic gratification, pure and simple.

How far is oedipal guilt and depth being replaced by the surfaces, textures, and unidimensionality of a narcissistic, schizophrenic, present-focused culture? One of the problems with Madonna's and many women's sexuality on MTV is the excessive narcissism: Madonna clearly loves her own body, and she celebrates it, gleefully. To an extent, as I have shown, this is well and good as a model for young women. But what degree of female narcissism is beneficial? At what point does it veer into something negative? Utopian authors, like Camille Paglia, ignore how limited for self-development may be the encouragement in young women of excessive, narcissistic concern with their own bodies, their "look." I am not as pleased as Paglia to settle for the notion she attributes to Madonna that "we are nothing but masks." It might be preferable to help young women think about, and critique, the world they find themselves in, and to envision what contributions they might make to it.

Ultimately, the negative aspects of the new female culture are balanced by the new opportunities opened up by a form like the female rock videos discussed above. The negative dimensions of a return to an extreme sexism (albeit with women in a vastly different role) remain and must be carefully analyzed and addressed. At the same time teenage women are benefiting from being finally not only addressees in popular culture, but subjects who are actively producing and shaping it. The positive aspects of postmodernism are those which challenge earlier oppressive boundaries, rigid hierarchies, and fixed gender identities and sexualities. MTV in part offers a glimpse of a new social vision in which ethnic, gender, and class boundaries are transformed and relaxed, allowing a series of multiple subjectivities and individual possibilities.

REFERENCES

Baran, S. J. (1974). The effects of prosocial and antisocial television content on the modeling behavior of children with varying degrees of self-esteem. *Dissertation Abstracts International, 34*, 4069–4070.

Bloom, A. (1988). *The closing of the American mind.* New York: Harcourt Brace.

Brown, J. D., & Campbell, K. C. (1986). Race and gender in music videos: The same beat but a different drummer. *Journal of Communication, 36*, 94–106.

Brown, J. D., Schulze, L., Childers, K. W., & Nickopolou, L. (1988, October). Race and gender differences in interpretations of sexuality in music videos. Paper presented at the American Studies Association Conference, Miami, FL.

Brunsdon, C. (1983). Crossroads: Notes on soap opera. In E. A. Kaplan (Ed.) *Regarding television: Critical approaches—An anthology* (pp. 76–82). Los Angeles: American Film Institute.

Dent, G. (Ed.). (1992). *Black popular culture.* Seattle: Bay Press.

Diawara, M. (Ed.). (1991). Black cinema [Special issue]. *Wide Angle, 13.*

Doane, M. A. (1981). Woman's stake: Filming the female body. *October, 17,* 23–36.

Doane, M. A. (1987). *The desire to desire: The woman's films of the 1940s.* Bloomington: Indiana University Press.

Eron, L. O. (1982). Parent-child interaction, television violence and aggression of Children. *American Psychologist, 37,* 197–211.

Feuer, J. (1989). Reading *Dynasty*: Television and reception theory. *The South Atlantic Quarterly, 88,* 443–460.

Foucault, M. (1972). Discourse on language. *The Archeology of Knowledge.* A. M. Sheridan Smith (Trans.). New York: Pantheon.

Foucault, M. (1977). *Language, Counter-Memory, Practice.* D. F. Bouchard & S. Simon (Trans.). Ithaca, NY: Cornell University Press.

France, K. (1993, July 22). Grrrls at war. *Rolling Stone, 8,* 23.

Freedberg, D. (1989). *The power of images: Studies in the history and theory of response.* Chicago: University of Chicago Press.

Friedberg, A. (1990). A denial of difference: Theories of cinematic identification. In E. A. Kaplan (Ed.), *Psychoanalysis and cinema.* New York: Routledge.

Frith, S. (1981). *Sound effects: Youth, leisure, and the politics of rock and roll.* New York: Pantheon Books.

Gates, H. L., Jr. (1990, August 12). Article on "2 Live Crew," *New York Times.*

Gates, H. L., Jr. (Ed.). (1986). *Race, writing, and difference.* Chicago: University of Chicago Press.

Goad, D. (1993). Riot grrrls rrreally boring (sic). *Your Flesh, 29,* 22.

Hoffman, M. L. (1984). Moral development. In M. Lamb & M. Bornstein (Eds.). *Developmental psychology: An advanced textbook* (2nd ed., pp. 534–537). Hillsdale, NJ: Erlbaum.

Hooks, B. (1992). *Black looks: Race and representation.* Boston: South End Press.

Jameson, F. (1988). Postmodernism and the logic of late capital. In E. A. Kaplan (Ed.), *Postmodernism and its discontents: Theories and practices* (pp. 13–29). London: Verso. (Original work published 1984)

Johansson, T., & Miegel, F. (1992). *Do the right thing: Lifestyle and identity in contemporary youth culture.* Stockholm: Almquist & Wikseel.

Kaplan, E. A. (1987). *Rocking around the clock: Music Television postmodernism and consumer culture.* London: Routledge.

Kaplan, E. A. (1988). *Postmodernism and its discontents: Theories and practices.* London: Verso.

Kaplan, E. A. (1990a). Consuming images: Madonna and the 'look-alike'. In *Screen and monitor: Proceedings of conference* (pp. 41–67). Taiwan: Fu Jen University.

Kaplan, E. A. (1990b). Consuming images: The image and its rhetoric in USA culture and cultural studies. In *Screen and monitor: A critical investigation of image culture* (pp. 41–67). Taipei, Taiwan: Fu Jen University Press.

Kaplan, E. A. (1997). *Looking for the other: Feminism and the imperial gaze.* New York: Routledge.

Kaplan, E. A. (1990c). The sacred image of the same: Madonna/the look-alike/resistance. In *What a wonderful world! Music videos in architecture* (pp. 42–46). Groningen, Holland: The Groninger Museum.

Kaplan, E. A. (1992). *Motherhood and representation: The mother in popular culture and melodrama.* New York: Routledge.

Kaplan, E. A. (1993). Madonna: Masks or mastery? In C. Schwictenberg (Ed.), *The Madonna connection* (pp. 149–166). Boulder, CO: Westview Press.

Lewis, L. A. (1990). *Gender politics and MTV: Voicing the difference.* Philadelphia: Temple University Press.

Lovell, Terry. (1987). *Consuming fiction.* London: Verso.

Lowry, D. (1988). Nonverbal communication: A new perspective. In S. Hecker & D. Stewart (Eds.), *Nonverbal communication in advertising* (pp. 85–92). Lexington, MA: Lexington Books.

McRobbie, A. (1980). Settling accounts with subcultures: A feminist critique. *Screen Education, 34*, 37–49.

McRobbie, A., & Nava, M. (Eds.). (1984). *Gender and generation.* London: Macmillan.

Modleski, T. (1983). The rhythms of reception: Daytime television and women's work. In E. A. Kaplan (Ed.), *Regarding television* (pp. 65–77).

Mulvey, L. (1975). Visual pleasure and narrative cinema. *Screen, 16*, 6–18.

Mulvey, Laura. (1989). *Visual and other pleasures.* London: MacMillan.

Paglia, C. (1990, December 14). Madonna—finally, a real feminist. *New York Times,* Op. Ed. Page.

Plato. (1993). *Republic 5* (S. Halliwell, Trans.). Warminster, England: Aris & Philipps.

Postman, N. (1985). *Amusing ourselves to death: Public discourse in the age of show business.* New York: Viking.

Rimer, Sara. (1990, October 17). "Obscenity or Art? Trial on Rap Lyrics Opens." *New York Times,* pp. A1–A2

Roberts, R. (1996). *Ladies first: Women in music videos.* Jackson: University Press of Mississippi.

Schulze, L., White, A. B., & Brown, J. D. (1993). A sacred monster in her prime: Audience construction of Madonna as low-other. In C. Schwichtenberg (Ed.), *The Madonna connection: Representational politics, sub-cultural identities and cultural theory* (pp. 15–32). Boulder, CO: Westview Press.

Spender, Dale. (1986). *Mothers of the novel.* New York: Pandora

Wallace, M. (1990). *Invisibility blues: From pop to theory.* London: Routledge.

Watt, Ian. (1957). *The rise of the novel: Studies in Defoe, Richardson, and Fielding.* Berkeley: University of California Press.

Practice

5

The Pioneers of Media Psychology

Lilli Friedland and Fredrick Koenig

Media psychology has become a serious field of endeavor. The field encompasses a broad spectrum of psychologists who work with the media and play roles such as the following: developing the format and design for new technologies, consulting on script and character development for television and feature films; appearing as guest experts or hosts on radio and television shows, consulting to the print media or writing columns, consulting to news and talk programs or their guests and staff, and conducting research about the impact of different types of content or format on viewers.

Research in the field of media psychology (see Donnerstein & Smith, chapter 2, this volume) has even influenced public policy. For example, the 1996 Telecommunications Act mandated the installation of a V-chip, or violence chip, to help adults control the content of the programs that children watch. This action could have been predicated upon the research findings of psychologists.

Public interest in psychology has been great in recent years and this has encouraged the development of numerous talk shows in which psychologists have presented information to the public either through radio or TV. Many of the psychologists have become public personalities as a result of this exposure. In short, media psychology has become a significant force in psychology. It even has its own division within the American Psychological Association (APA), Division 46, which was launched in 1985. And the APA Public Affairs Office offers a list of qualified media psychologists who are frequently interviewed by the print, radio, and television media.

What are the roots of this unique field? As Kutner points out (see chapter 7, this volume) psychologists began to appear in the media as early as the 1920s. But it was in the 1970s and 1980s, corresponding with the rising popularity of "call-in talk radio," that radio and television programs started regularly including psychologists as guests and hosts. In order to better understand how psychologists came to enter the field of media psychology, we interviewed some of the pioneer media psychologists about their experiences. We asked Joyce Brothers, Sonya Friedman, Pat and Barry Bricklin, Toni Grant, Joy Brown, and Larry Balter to respond to a structured questionnaire (see Appendix). This chapter presents highlights of their interviews but does not contain citations as this chapter is the first attempt to chronicle the history of the pioneers.

Joyce Brothers

While teaching at Hunter College and Columbia University, I found I could teach only a few students. All the information that could make people's lives easier if they had access to it was locked up in the library. Also, so much of what was in the library was incomprehensible to the average individual because one would have to study for such a long time to understand these ideas. I decided I wanted to teach psychology to a larger group and chose to use the media.

I went to Metropolitan Education Television in New York and offered the psychology course I was developing. They accepted and the course was aired at 6:00 A.M. I then decided to talk to the local NBC television station about teaching at a time when people would be listening. They agreed to give me a firm four week contract in August 1959. What they wanted was what we now have on air—people with their coats open and cuts on their necks, saying, "I already tried to commit suicide." I said, "No way." Nonetheless, the show was very successful and I wound up with two programs, one at 1:00 P.M. and then another a few minutes after the Jack Parr Show. Then the show went into syndication with ABC in 1966. In 1960 I had also started a radio show while working at the NBC network and also for the local NBC station. I have been doing the NBC radio/Westwood 1 Network continuously since then. The programs I do are short reports about what people don't know about themselves.

I didn't know a soul in "the business." I just went in cold into the networks and asked them to have such a program. I was the first; in essence I invented the field. Now it is so successful that there is a media psychologist in most large cities.

I believe it is helpful for people to see the face of psychologists—to see that psychologists don't have horns and green teeth, that they are friendly and have a sense of humor. Many people have said that I have made psychologists friendly to the audience. When I started in this field, people felt that they had to be crazy to go for help. It has changed so that now people feel it is O.K. to go to therapy for problems with everyday life.

I don't see any liabilities for psychologists who work with the media. It is important for psychologists to speak in their area of expertise. As long as they are comfortable with their training and their commitment to the profession of psychology, they will do well. The problem is with those who wear the mantle of psychologists but aren't properly trained or people who are psychotherapists and the public think they are psychologists. It is very important for psychologists to make clear to the public who is credentialed or licensed and who isn't.

My goal is to continue in my own way to be certain that what I do is honorable and that I am careful about quoting correct facts.

Sonya Friedman

I have been in print media, newspapers, magazines, and books, written a couple of regular newspaper columns, and also have been involved in both radio and television.

Outside events and internal motivation prompted personal involvement in the field of media psychology. This began right after I received a PhD in psychology from Wayne State University. I noticed that a local newspaper, called the *Eccentric*, did not have a psychological column. This prompted me to call the editor and to offer my services. When he asked me whether I had any experience writing I told him I had written a doctoral dissertation. He informed me that it and a dime would get me a phone call. I remembered responding, "Why not give the kid a chance?" I offered to write six columns for him and he didn't have to pay me. I said, "If you like them, you can use them and we could arrange payment." I wrote for that paper for years for the grand sum of $10 a column.

I then had an opportunity to write for the *Detroit Free Press*, and I wrote that weekly column for almost ten years for $100 per column. In one of my pieces I had used the word "orgasm" making a remark that, "If she is smiling up at you then you know for sure she is not having one." At the time, that column was considered quite risqué and was picked by the local ABC station for a segment on their morning talk show. The producers and I got along well and I was then invited back for a weekly segment on that show. From there, I became the resident psychologist in Detroit, Cleveland, New York, and Chicago for the ABC morning shows and AM America.

Having known a lot of the folks at ABC, I was then introduced to the head of the news division. He offered me an opportunity to do a news segment. The first one I did, which was an experiment, was on the 40+ club. This was a story about men who lose their jobs in mid-life. Later, I was hired to be a special correspondent doing stories on social issues on the evening news with Barbara Walters and Harry Reasoner. I left after 2 1/2 years because I didn't feel I was earning my keep and I wasn't improving my journalistic skills as rapidly as I wanted. I came back to Detroit and received a call from the head of a local talk-radio station. He claimed he had listened to my voice on television and he thought I had a good voice for radio. He asked me to consider being a talk-radio psychologist in Detroit. After about eight years on-air in Detroit, I was hired by the ABC network. I flew to New York two days a week to do the radio show which was then beamed around the country. Later, I was hired by CNN to host my own television show, which I also did for almost eight years. In addition to that show I did a number of public service and local programs.

My experience has been very broad-based. I have to be honest and say that I was there at the right time in what was a very limited field on radio and television. My career just expanded without any great intention. I did not have an agent. It was just one of those things in which doors opened and I said yes. It's been a delight being able to perform. It was fueled by a deep-seated sense that speaking to people on the air was like being with folks in my office except that it was done in public. It was a good opportunity to share some critical information and I was pleased to be the one to be given this honor and responsibility.

In the historical evolution of media psychology, I was among the first on-air psychologists along with Toni Grant and Joy Browne. I don't know of any psychologist that was hired before me for national news. Though CNN hired me, I never felt they made effective use of my psychological knowledge.

The benefits of having psychologists in the media are enormous and yet they have not been adequately utilized. Psychologists in the media can show the public how the world impacts on people and how people impact on the world. It is possible to draw correlations between a variety of things that either impact on or relate to each other; or show how a certain event is the sum of a number of parts and variables that were working together. Psychologists can also give people choices which they may not have had because of lack of information or inappropriate role models. Despite these potential benefits, the use of psychologists by the media is relatively small.

The liability of having psychologists involved with the media are only the liabilities of the individual psychologists. Some psychologists misuse their opportunities. For example, a few people have not done their homework or have said things that weren't true. Other psychologists appear on air simply for their own self-aggrandizement or economics. There are some who try to build a practice by giving their own telephone numbers on the air as a regular routine. I think to do so once in a while is not horrible, but to do so regularly is to advertise, which is inappropriate.

Another problem area is when psychologists become instant experts. It would be wonderful if people would feel comfortable enough to express their knowledge and yet refer to someone else in those areas in which they aren't expert. There is also the liability when someone does a poor job, or is dull or dull-witted. That type of performance does reflect poorly on the profession as a whole.

I am always interested when psychologists are selling a book. For example, we know that their public relations person tells them to say the title of the book. Certainly their publisher wants that. Yet, there are ways to interview in which you are not just out there selling your product. You have to make it clear that your product is there to help people and not just for your own ego.

I think it is important not to become a star. One of the things we all realize is that family keeps us grounded. We are real people and not everyone will love us. We are going to be criticized. As opposed to developing thick skins, I think we can develop a more quizzical attitude so that negative comments can help us to take a look about what we are doing. Sometimes criticism happens because of the jealousy of our colleagues, and one always has to be prepared for that. Sometimes it happens because we really do present in an arrogant or cavalier way. I think that psychologists have to temper the belief that television makes them larger than life and that books make them real experts. You must remember that you have the same problems with your spouse and children as everyone else does.

Organized psychology got in my way with great regularity. I would hear from people in the profession who criticized my being on radio. A technique that I always used to take care of that was to call them and invite them on the show and ten out of ten came. Not one of them who criticized what I was doing, or said that she or he felt negative about what I was doing refused to share the platform with me. This reaction told me a great deal about what was going on. I also had some psychologists who offered to substitute for me when I was on vacation and who clearly were trying to get the job for themselves. One, in fact whom I suggested as a substitute, had her agent call to offer her as a replacement for me. That made me kind of sad. I would have been happy to share without putting myself out of business.

There was also a very interesting incident with the Ohio Psychological Association, which contacted me after I was a regular guest on a very well-known show saying that I was not licensed to practice in Ohio. I responded by saying I was not practicing psychology; I was educating and teaching by giving information. I have not heard any more about that.

Pat and Barry Bricklin

Pat

In 1965, I was invited to appear on a radio call-in show. With some reluctance, I accepted the invitation and found to my surprise that I enjoyed the experience and found it a real challenge to communicate psychological information simply and clearly in nontechnical language. I did not know it, but this particular program spot was used to audition psychologists for a continuing program. At that time each of the CBS owned stations throughout the country planned to have its own daily psychology program. During the interview with the program director following my appearance on the program, I mentioned that my husband, Barry was also a psychologist.

Pat and Barry

We began to explore the option of doing the program as a husband/wife professional couple. Up to that time there were few psychologists in the media and they were not well received by their peers. At the same time, the opportunity to do a responsible and thoughtful job and to explore new avenues for professional psychology were there. We decided to take the risk. We began five years of daily radio shows which started as half-hour programs and were extended to an hour and a half as they grew in popularity. This was followed by a year of daily television shows and finally a weekly radio program which extended into the 1980s.

As psychologists in the media before media psychology existed as a legitimate area of concentration for psychologists, we found ourselves confronting a number of personal, professional, and ethical issues for which clear guidelines did not exist. These issues revolved around the following: working as a team, our responsibilities to the profession of psychology, ethical dilemmas, our responsibilities to our listeners, and the organization and communication of psychological content.

We considered two major questions as they related to our responsibility to the profession: First, should psychologists be involved in the media at all, particularly in listener participation programs? Second, is it possible for psychologists to participate in such programs in a professionally responsible and ethical manner which enhances psychology? Both of us believed that the answer to both of these questions was "yes." Initially the attitudes of our peers were variable. All of the ethical committees of the various medical and psychiatric societies reviewed audio tapes of our programs for possible professional and ethical lapses. Although we were already highly sensitive to ethical and professional responsibility, this early constant monitoring by our peers certainly sharpened our awareness and gave us early firsthand experience with peer review. For example, it was clear that it would have been unethical and professionally irresponsible for us to use our media recognizability as a mechanism for increasing our own independent practices. In response to the frequently asked question: "How can I get to see you?" we would offer other sources of appropriate referral information.

Another source of pressure came from some of our sponsors who asked us to be spokespersons for their products. We also had to deal with the recurrent ethical issue of what types of products or services were appropriate as sponsors for "on air" psychologists.

The most difficult and continuous dilemma for us was the ethical principle which at that time prohibited personal advice in the media. For the most part, we helped to provide our listeners with the kind of information upon which they could base informed decisions. We worked through questions and answers, analogies and illustrations to clarify unclear or distorted beliefs or feelings that stood in the way of intelligent decision-making. From time to time, we gave personal advice because withholding it would, in our opinion, have been unethical and irresponsible.

In addition to the 'personal advice' dilemma, the need to balance the ethical principles of autonomy (the right of the person to self direction) and beneficence (motivation to do what is best for a person, to help others) was ever present. At times they conflicted, just as they do in independent psychotherapeutic practice.

Communicating information accurately and clearly to diminish the opportunities for distortion was always a primary aim and responsibility. Providing our listeners with access to a network of appropriate referral sources was clearly a continuing responsibility. We never made referrals to specific individual professionals, but rather, provided the way to tap into a network of providers.

Over time, we noted an increase in public awareness and sophistication about psychology. There was a shift in our "on the air" callers from an emphasis on child and family problems to a focus on the self and intimate relationships.

Our notions about therapy and specific therapeutic strategies also underwent dramatic shifts as a direct result of our media work. Our ideas were critically scrutinized by both our professional colleagues and our listeners. This kind of ongoing review and comment was incredibly valuable.

In 1981, because of other commitments, we completed our media work. The experience of working in the media was an experience of making a difference as dual advocates both for psychology and for consumers of psychological services.

Toni Grant

My broadcasting career began in 1972 when I met Bill Ballance at a New Year's Eve party. Bill had been hosting a show geared toward women called "The Feminine Forum" and it had been very successful. Times were changing, however; the feminist movement was at its height and women were demanding more serious and informative programming. In an effort to address this issue, Bill started to invite weekly cohosts whom he called his "resident sages," primarily psychologists and psychiatrists. He was tremendously encouraging, and I spent three years in this capacity. When the show was canceled, however, I realized that I did not want to return to full time private practice. Broadcasting was a natural for me; my mother was a Montessori teacher who specialized in speech and drama, and her influence had been profound. In addition, I strongly believed that many of the people who sought psychotherapy were simply in need of information and guidance; it was clear to me that a lot of dysfunctional behavior was simply what behaviorists call a "learning deficit." In those days, psychology as a profession was still very much "in the closet"; people really didn't know exactly what a psychologist "did." I wanted to demystify our profession and bring it out into the open. I viewed the media as a wonderful, educational opportunity.

At that time, there was no such thing as "media psychology" and there was no one on the air who was doing this sort of thing full time. When I approached the station executives about this prospect, they were initially skeptical about the entertainment value of a straight psychology call-in show and worried that it would be "too depressing" for daytime. To allay their fears and prove myself, I accepted the overnight 12:00 A.M. to 5:00 A.M. shift, a schedule which actually worked extremely well in terms of my family. The show was an almost instant success and within a year was moved to afternoon prime time. As the ratings soared, hundreds of radio stations across the country started to use our format.

"The Dr. Toni Grant Program" went into national syndication in 1981. In 1985, after 10 wonderful years with KABC in Los Angeles and the ABC Radio Network, I decided to make a change and moved to Westwood One/Mutual Broadcasting System where I stayed until 1990.

My radio career was an exciting and fulfilling one which suited my personality, my background, and my life goals and aspirations. I wanted to make a difference in the world, and I think I did. My aim was to educate, to enlighten, and to inspire people in their life and in their work. I always felt that my true gift was teaching rather than clinical practice but I never expected to do it quite this way. What a wonderful classroom it was! I got a great deal of love back from the public whom I served, and this, too, was extremely gratifying; most clinicians have to wait a long time to get the stroking which they deserve. I suspect they may be a great deal more patient than I.

As for problems which I experienced in the media, there were relatively few. It was often frustrating to move as quickly as management liked and there was always a certain amount of conflict about this. I tried to stay close to the research, made a lot of on and off the air referrals, and recommended a great number of self-help books. The bottom line for management, of course, was ratings, and my challenge was to be as entertaining as possible while still being informative and helpful.

Over the course of 15 years I could feel the pulse of the culture changing, and as it changed, I changed my focus to suit the mood and the need of the times. In the 70's there was a great deal of emphasis on personal autonomy and independence: issues of finding one's self, developing one's own identity, going back to school, assertiveness training, that sort of thing. By the mid 80's this had begun to change, and callers became more concerned with issues of commitment, interdependence, and family values. On a personal level, I shared the same yearnings as many of my listeners, and began a spiritual and intellectual journey which culminated in the publication of my book *Being A Woman* (Random House, 1988). The book, subtitled "Fulfilling Your Femininity And Finding Love," urged a return a traditional feminine values and morals.

It is interesting to note that as society became more permissive, people began to turn to psychologists for guidance on how to live, rather than to their churches or synagogues. But psychologists have not been very responsive to this need. Traditionally, psychologists have been reluctant to deal with moral dilemmas, that is, issues of right or wrong. While I understand the clinical reasons for this, I strongly believe that man has a spiritual dimension to his nature which must be acknowledged, developed, and shaped. I have found the writings of Carl Jung and his followers extremely helpful in developing my thinking in this area. Cognitive therapy and behavior modification can be used to show people that they can indeed control their own behavior and thinking, and act in accordance with their deepest values in spite of their prior conditioning. I feel there is an urgent need in our current culture for psychologists to be more proactive in this arena.

Following my marriage, I took a break from broadcasting to "live the book I wrote." This hiatus has been personally and professionally very enriching. I took some time off and then entered the corporate world where I greatly expanded my knowledge of business and the workplace. The most critical learning, however, has occurred on a personal and intimate level, and I am eager to share this knowledge with the public. I am first and foremost a media psychologist; this has been my life's work. I hope I have represented our profession well, and plan to return to the airwaves in the near future.

Joy Browne

In 1978, I got a message from my answering service to call "WITS." I didn't know what a WITS was, but I'm really good about returning phone calls. When I reached them, Harold Bausmer, the general sales manager, said that my name kept popping up when they interviewed area psychologists (88 at that moment) and was I interested in doing a talk show? I had no idea what a talk show was. When he explained to me, I said, "Nope, all I have to market is my reputation and it means nothing to anybody but me, but it's all I have." He asked if I was willing to have lunch and talk about it. Because I had to pick up my daughter, I agreed to a quick cup of coffee during which I hoped to be obnoxious or at least contentious enough to extinguish their enthusiasm, forgetting that men often take no as a challenge. When I got tired of being sorta rude, I agreed to appear once as a guest during which time a caller found out from me that he could not have been a sociopath because he'd married, had kids, held a job, never been arrested, and wasn't violent. You could hear him put down years of sadness and I thought, "hum..." and I've been doing it ever since.

A friend convinced me at the time that if I could help 300 people in a year, I could do that in a day on the air (he was off by several orders of magnitude, because I now reach between 3 and 5 million listeners a day); as a do-gooder, unrepentant I might add. Pretty seductive stuff. After three years in Boston at WITS, I got an offer I couldn't refuse from KGO in San Francisco and actually spent a year doing news because I wanted to see if the fun was broadcast or psychology. I found out very quickly the fun was psychology (news makes people miserable and what I do, in theory, makes people feel better, at least eventually). I loathed doing the news. Three years later ABC in New York beckoned and then ABC nationally. I went to Daynet directly from ABC when ABC folded their talk division, literally without a break. I then went to WOR in New York and the WOR radio network on which I currently have 280 affiliates.

Having done this longer than anybody currently on the air (Toni Grant preceded me but left before I did. Well, I haven't left yet, have I?), I have maintained from day one that although it's fun, being on the air on a daily basis cannot and should not be combined with a private practice. Once you go public, I don't think you can be private simultaneously. Therapy is a powerful tool and you don't want people coming in to see what you look like, to brag who their therapist is, or to think they can solve a problem in five minutes.

Initially, I did not enjoy the current position of teaching other psychologists to take my job, as I have done at every national conference for the past ten years in addition to serving on the board of the division. In fact, my first year on the air, the Massachusetts division asked me to deliver a speech at their convention and had ten people from the ethics committee in town to pull my license. Once I tumbled to the fact that I wasn't exactly being honored, I explained that when you say psychologist most Americans think either Bob Newhart, an actor, or Joyce Brothers, whose license was pulled years ago. I pointed out that the show was popular so the issue wasn't whether or not it would be on, but whether good and ethical people who had some real connection to psychology would be doing the work or unethical charlatans who were in it to entertain exclusively rather than educate. I did then and continue to welcome feedback from other psychologists. Even at that meeting it was amazing how many of these naysayers wanted me to have their card in case I needed a substitute host. I had no objection to their initial reservations since I also had them, but none of them had even bothered to listen to the program.

I continue to feel that there is a true and good job of educating the public that can be done by being nonthreatening, nonjudgmental, and accessible, not to mention free. By demystifying the field, hopefully we really are able to take it to the people. I would have loved to have a role model, feedback, and colleagues with whom to discuss my concerns, which is why I stay active with APA. In spite of early misgivings, APA and I have decided we can help each other, or at least they have decided I can be useful.

For those intrepid souls who are considering entering the field of media, and I know there are lots because it seems glamorous, let me warn you, it will change your life in lots of ways, some fun, some not so fun, but I truly think you have to give up the idea of a private practice while you are doing the work. I would truly like to be less public; getting recognized on a date or asked for an autograph when you're trying to have a serious discussion, or someone asking for your picture—not to mention mash notes—is disconcerting to say the least. It is hard to imagine less disparate goals than the quiet, private life of a practitioner and the noisy, public one of a media shrink. People feel you're their best friend and you've never met them, death threats are unanticipated problems, and when I speak, I have to be careful not to mouth off because my words take on more significance than I would like. You truly have to give up casual comments let alone sarcasm or smart alecky rejoinders.

On the other hand, the outpouring of feelings and gratitude and the process that you can occasionally hear over the air make it fun and exciting. And I do love the movie premieres.

Lawrence Balter

As a professor at New York University, I was approached by the Public Affairs Office of APA about becoming a contributor to a local all-news radio station. The Dean of the law school and others were also asked to contribute brief pre-recorded pieces to be aired at various times during the day. I wrote a couple of pieces for a two-three minute segment called "Let's Talk Psychology," and they were accepted. For several years thereafter, I recorded pieces on psychology in a question and answer format with the news anchors at the station. From that point forward I was hooked on the media!

The first media psychologist was Dr. Joyce Brothers. At that time, the profession did not look favorably upon her work. She told me that if I pursued a career in the media, I would probably have to choose between professional colleagues and the public. Another media psychologist at the time was Dr. Lee Salk. I was particularly aware of his work because it was in the same area as mine, namely, parent–child relationships. At times we appeared on panels together. At other times we competed for employment in the media.

I have worked in all areas of the media: television, radio, books, and magazines. After I entered the field of media psychology with my appearances on the local news radio station, I had the opportunity to offer an educational TV program on the CBS television network. It was presented in conjunction with New York University and was called *Sunrise Semester*. The program was designed for teachers and was offered for college credit. My course was called "Discipline in the Classroom." Though the production values were quite limited, I learned a great deal about standing in front of a camera and acting "natural."

My next step was public affairs television through NYU. I got to appear on NBC TV-owned and -operated stations with a program that I coproduced and moderated called "Children and All That Jazz." I received a media award from the APA for this program. Because of the media exposure I was receiving, I was asked to appear on many radio and television shows. As I honed my skills, opportunities increased.

My first break into commercial media came when I was hired by WABC Talk radio in New York to host my own call-in program for parents. The management called me to come into the radio station at midnight. I could not imagine that my audition would be live in the middle of the night. But it was. Much to my surprise, the telephone lines lit up and weary parents asked all sorts of questions about their children. A new career was born. I was hired to host my own program every Saturday and Sunday morning from 9:00 A.M. to noon and remained on air for several years. After a couple of years, the program was expanded to the ABC Talk radio network. In the mid-80s, I was hired to serve as the resident child psychologist on the CBS TV morning news. I appeared regularly on that show for several years until it was canceled.

Around the same time, I became a Contributing Editor and wrote a regular column on parenting for *Ladies' Home Journal*. I remain a Contributing Editor to this magazine as well as a Contributing Editor and columnist at *Sesame Street Parents*. I have also written a series of eight books for preschool age children, as well as books on parenting.

In 1987, I was hired by WABC TV in New York as a feature reporter for their Eyewitness News program. I appeared several times each week for five years and hosted a special on children and sports. Subsequently, I worked for several years with *Home*, an ABC TV network magazine program, as an expert in the area of child rearing and parenting. I currently appear on the weekend edition of *Today* on NBC TV and on the weekend *Eyewitness News* on WABC TV in New York.

Later in my career, a group of us who had been on radio and TV got together on a monthly basis to discuss career problems and strategies. These meetings were helpful. Many individuals were exceedingly helpful in my acquisition of presentation skills. However, they worked in various branches of the media, not in psychology. Psychologists entering the field today are fortunate in that they can be trained by other media psychologists. Now I find myself counseling countless psychologists who are interested in becoming involved in the media.

There are many benefits to the public in having psychologists involved in the media. First, it increases the likelihood that interpretations of psychological principles will be valid and accurate. Second, it brings to public awareness the work of psychologists. I suspect that most people do not know what psychologists actually do in their labs, classes, and offices. Exposure in the media can help remove many mistaken beliefs on the part of the lay public.

Psychologists are involved in the media in a variety of ways. Many do not appear in the media but lend their expertise to the various media. Numerous psychologists work with computer programs, conduct research on the effects of media, consult on scripts, and serve as experts reviewing content for television and print material.

Psychologists who appear in print or TV must abide by the highest ethical standards and be up-to-date on the latest research and clinical methods. There are potential liabilities. If the psychologist is eager for exposure, for personal gain, there is the risk that she or he might compromise professional standards and therefore serve as a poor representative of the profession. When a psychologist "shoots from the hip" in interviews, or serves on panels with inadequate preparation, or confuses polemic with research data, problems can arise.

I think my personal life was both enriched and strained by my work as a media psychologist. On the one hand, recognition by the public can be wonderfully soothing to one's vanity, but it also requires that one conduct oneself in a prudent manner even when one is not "on." I have found the work in media to be rewarding in several ways. I have learned more about child rearing problems than I ever could have from books or my clinical practice alone. My radio programs enabled me to talk to thousands of parents and to hear a myriad of problems that occur daily with children. At the same time, I found it a personally rewarding experience to be helpful to so many people. Media work has also forced me to increase my knowledge of psychological techniques and research in a wide variety of areas, which has broadened my insight into human behavior.

A cautionary note to others who might become involved with careers in the media: Individuals who appear in the media can be swept up in the "star" mentality. Too many who bask in the glow of the spotlight become spoiled. They develop an exaggerated sense of their worth and abilities. Their careers turn from a focus on being in a helping profession to that of self-aggrandizement.

When I first became involved in media there were only a few psychologists active in radio and television. I recall speaking with Dr. Joyce Brothers early on. She had trouble with the profession when she first started out in media. I think she felt that she was forced to make a choice between her professional colleagues and the public. In a sense, I think she was ahead of her time.

My experience has been different. Media psychologists are now much more accepted by their professional peers. And by restricting my media work only to areas of expertise and presenting myself as a professional, I believe I have earned the respect of my professional colleagues. Recently I was invited to discuss the value of interacting with the media with my University faculty colleagues and the American Psychological Association awarded me a national media award.

Psychologists can become involved in the latest areas of the media, namely computer technology. The Internet, for example, offers a challenge to psychologists in many ways. We can contribute to a greater understanding of the social psychological impact of on-line communication. We can offer expert advice on the application of computer technology to education, job performance, and child development. Psychology can begin to explore the use of advanced computer technology in the areas of diagnosis and amelioration of clinical problems.

Psychologists can also use the media to increase the public awareness of children's needs and proper parenting strategies. Through the media, we can offer behavioral solutions. In short, psychologists in the media can help society in a number of important ways.

Conclusion

These trailblazing pioneers broke ground for all of the media psychologists of today. Risking professional censure, they dared to take the first steps needed to give psychology away to the public at large. There were no mentors or guideposts for these trailblazers, as they were the first group in the field. They expressed a sense of loneliness and wanting more contact and conversation with their colleagues, especially in the early days. Yet, they all succeeded in their vision of sharing their knowledge and expertise with a larger number of individuals through the media rather than limiting it to the few that could be reached in the traditional office setting. In the end all of them expressed tremendous satisfaction with being "on air."

These pioneers stressed the importance of exquisite attention to ethics and the need to consult with respected psychologists to ensure the maintenance of the highest professional standards. They cautioned against going beyond the limits of one's expertise or being swallowed up by the pursuit of the limelight. But they all indicated that when one acts ethically, carefully, and with integrity one can learn, grow, and have a deeply gratifying experience as a media psychologist. They strongly encouraged other psychologists to work in the field.

The interviewees also stressed the incredible benefits of having psychologists in the media, benefits that include the dissemination of knowledge about people and the world, the opening up of personal and social understanding, public access to more choices, and public education about psychotherapy and more. They point to an even richer future for media psychologists—a future in which psychologists will work in a variety of new arenas that will be created by the interactive technologies of the next century. These remarkable pioneers opened the door for all of us and now welcome others to a field that is ripe with possibilities for personal satisfaction and public benefit.

Appendix

Media Psychology Questionnaire

1. What outside events and what internal motivation prompted your personal involvement in media psychology? (A personal historical perspective would be helpful.)
2. From your perspective, how would you describe the historical evolution of media and psychology? When did this start? Who were the chief players? When did you enter the field? What role did you play?
3. From your perspective, what are the benefits of having psychologists involved in the media? You may be as specific or general as you wish.
4. From your perspective, what are the liabilities of having psychologists involved in the media? You may be as specific or general as you wish.
5. What was the impact on your personal life of being involved in the media? What cautions would you recommend to other psychologists who get involved with the media?
6. When you contemplated getting involved in the media did you discuss or get advice or support from others who were already involved? Did you have a mentor? If yes, whom and what role did she or he play in guiding you? If not, do you wish you had a mentor? What role do you wish she or he had played?
7. Did individual psychologists or organized psychologists discourage or get in the way of your involvement with the media? If so, how? Were there effective methods for turning them around to becoming supportive of your media psychology efforts?

8. From your perspective do you see individual psychologists or organized psychology not facilitating the role of psychology or psychologists in the media? If so, please describe.
9. What opportunities would you like to see media psychologists pursue in the future? How do see this happening? What role would you like to play in shaping the future of media psychology?

6

The Voice of America:
Culturally Sensitive Radio

Florence W. Kaslow

The first portion of this chapter is devoted to a short rendition of how the Voice of America (VOA), the broadcasting arm of the United States Information Agency (USIA), was established, its history, and its purposes. The remainder of the chapter discusses a specific program on VOA, the first that is psychological in nature in VOA's entire 54 year history. It is written primarily in the first person since it describes a personal experience, and this is what was invited by the volume's editors.

Voice of America: Radio Broadcasts
Around the World

VOA came into being in 1942. Since then it has become one of the largest news gathering organizations in the world. The combined VOA installations function 24 hours a day, 365 days a year, and are capable of relaying news and other information instantaneously to millions of listeners worldwide across the airwaves. There are approximately 1,855 VOA staffers who come from over 60 countries; they are located in the United States and at overseas stations, so this is a mammoth enterprise (Bureau of Broadcasting, 1993).

"The news may be good. The news may be bad. We shall tell you the truth," said announcer William Harlan Hale during the first VOA broadcast in German on February 24, 1942—just 2 1/2 months after the United States entered World War II. During the war, VOA operated under the Office of War Information, but it was moved to the Department of State when the war ended. VOA became part of the USIA in 1953 when it was established to carry out the overseas information and cultural exchange programs of the U.S. government. This is where it remains today.

For the past 54 years, VOA has earned a reputation for providing up-to-the-minute, accurate, and balanced news, features, and music to its international audience. In recent decades, as rapid changes have been occurring in many parts of the globe, the need for understanding and the exchange of information in a larger number of fields of endeavor has become greater than ever before. VOA not only provides millions of listeners of every race, religion, nationality, and socioeconomic status with trustworthy, reliable, and comprehensive news of happenings in the United States, their own country, and the wide world outside their borders, but also offers practical and important information about how to build and maintain new democracies and free market economies (VOA, 1995).

Although there are approximately 125 similar broadcast services worldwide, VOA is considered one of the top three international broadcasters in today's vast global media market, along with BBC World Service and Radio Moscow. Ninety-two million listeners tune in VOA programs in 47 languages via direct medium wave (AM) and shortwave broadcasts. Millions more listen to VOA programs on their local AM and FM stations. Thus VOA serves a vast global community (USIA, 1995).

VOA publicity indicates that to be effective, VOA must gain the attention and respect of listeners (Bureau of Broadcasting, 1993). Thus, the principles governing its broadcasts are as follows:

1. VOA will serve as a consistently reliable and authoritative source of news. VOA news will be accurate, objective, and comprehensive.

2. VOA will represent America as multidimensional, rather than unidimensional, and therefore will present a balanced and comprehensive projection of significant American thought and institutions.
3. VOA will present the policies of the United States clearly and effectively, and also will present responsible discussions and opinion on these policies.

VOA's mission is to be an intellectual lifeline of credible information for its overseas audience in times of peace, war, and political upheaval. It is on the scene to report the news as it happens. More than 80 writers and editors in VOA's Newsroom and 40 correspondents at 25 news bureaus in the United States and throughout the world write, update, and report an average of 200 news stories each day. Part-time "stringers" file additional reports in English and many of the other languages VOA uses, expanding the range of breaking stories.

Approximately 59% of all VOA programming is news; another 26% comprises feature programs about economics, science, agriculture, medicine, sports, and American history and culture. Music from jazz and rock to classical and country constitutes 12%, and editorials make up the remaining 3% of the programming. VOA also produces special English programs, "Tuning in the USA" and "English USA," to help listeners improve their English skills.

In 1985, VOA began offering its programs to local AM and FM radio stations everywhere. Today, VOA programs ranging from satellite-delivered programs to radio bridges to partnership broadcasts are transmitted on satellite circuits to over 1,000 independently owned stations in 188 countries. A network of relay stations in the United States and overseas transmits programs across oceans and continents to an international audience via satellite, shortwave, and AM. The connection is instantaneous, even though the signal must pass through several different channels before it reaches the receiver. VOA operates relay stations in places like Botswana, Germany, Greece, Kuwait, Morocco, Philippines, Sri Lanka, and Thailand, as well as Delano, California, and Greenville, North Carolina.

The VOA Charter was drafted in 1960 but not signed into law (Public Law 94-350) until July 12, 1976, by then President Gerald Ford. Eighteen years later, on April 30, 1994, President Clinton signed the United States International Broadcasting Act, combining for the first time all U.S. government international broadcast services under a Board of Governors. The Board oversees the operations of VOA and three surrogate international broadcast services—Radio Free Europe, Radio Liberty, and the proposed Radio Free Asia, which was established under the new legislation. VOA will remain a U.S. government entity, and the other three will be grantee organizations. VOA received approximately $215 million for operating expenses from Congress in 1995.

The Parenting Corner

In the spring of 1993 I received a phone call from Irina Burgener, Special Events Coordinator at VOA. She indicated that one of the members of the Russian section broadcasting team had recently been back to her native country and had noticed the enormous changes that Russian families were experiencing due to the mammoth alterations in the Russian sociopolitical and economic systems. These reflected the upheaval wrought by the transformation from a communist to a capitalist society and enterprise system. The reporter thought that a program focusing on parent–child interactions, which would zero in on the new kinds of conflicts arising as a result of changes occurring in family dynamics and structure, could prove extremely beneficial. Specifically, the staff hoped that the program would enable parents to cope more effectively with their increasingly outspoken and rebellious children. They were seeking a family psychologist who had traveled and lectured in Eastern Europe and elsewhere, and who had a broad grasp of family issues from a multicultural perspective. They also preferred someone with media experience.

When they solicited recommendations from several sources, my name was given to them as that of someone who met the specifications. The caller asked, "Are you interested?" Immediately and somewhat impulsively I responded "absolutely." Intuitively it sounded like a wonderful new venue in which to "give psychology away," and through which to reach a huge untapped audience and perhaps help to improve their turbulent lives.

Locating the "Experts"

Shortly thereafter, I received a call from Irene Kelner, MD, PhD, the person who originated the idea for the show and who had gotten it approved through VOA. Dr. Kelner had over a decade of experience on VOA reporting news of fast breaking world events and had several featured programs each week, particularly on medical information. She indicated that she had attended and reported on international conferences on HIV and AIDS and was interested in this phenomenon from a psychological as well as a medical perspective. She had become increasingly concerned about the difficulties wrought by the changes in the way families are perceived and are functioning, and about the dearth of psychological services for children and families in contemporary Russia. Dr. Kelner believed a carefully crafted series of programs geared to imparting knowledge and "how to" suggestions would be well received and valued.

In the course of a few phone conversations, we exchanged background information to determine if we thought we could work together. I learned that Dr. Kelner had received her medical degree from the First Moscow Medical School (now Moscow Medical Academy), and her PhD in immunology from the Central Institute of Hematology in the former Soviet Union before she emigrated to the United States. After coming to the United States, she conducted research in molecular biology and taught histology at Case Western University Medical School. From there she went to the National Cancer Institute at the National Institutes of Health (NIH) in Washington, DC., where she took postdoctoral training and did research in cancer immunology. Later she became founder and director of the International Children's Leukemia Association. In 1982 she joined the staff of VOA as an International Radio broadcaster, with responsibilities for programs in (a) health and medicine, (b) principles of management, (c) business, and (d) parenting. She has received several VOA Awards for Excellence in Programming and derives much gratification from being able to disseminate relevant, current information to her "target audience" in Russia.

Dr. Kelner explained that each of our programs would be done by phone from the VOA broadcasting studio to my home or office. Each segment would be taped and then edited by her and translated into Russian. The tapes would then be broadcast on shortwave as part of VOA programs in the Russian language. Also, they would be sent to the various VOA affiliate stations in Russia and other republics of the former Soviet Union, including Armenia, Estonia, Georgia, Kazakhstan, Kyrgystan, and Ukraine. Currently the VOA Russian service has 24 affiliates in the former USSR.

She indicated that programs done by one VOA service can be adopted and adapted by services going to other countries and used in English, translated into the language of that region, or done with voice-overs.

Dr. Kelner opined that numerous services probably would be interested and therefore the program would have wide distribution and many secondary target audiences. She indicated that this would be the first continuous program series on VOA Russian service that was psychological in nature. I found the total package appealing. The fact that it was made clear at the outset that VOA has no funds available for guests on such programs, and that all of the work would therefore be pro bono, seemed congruent with their "mission" and mine.

In turn, I shared a little about my background, particularly such facts as my long-standing interest in an international perspective in my personal and professional life. I told Dr. Kelner that my husband and I served for years as a host family for foreign students through the International House in Philadelphia—hosting and becoming extended family to students from such diverse countries as Korea, the Philippines, India, and Mexico. We served as sponsors when our Indian student's family decided to apply for American citizenship. As our children approached their teen years and we were free to travel, I began in 1974 to be invited to guest lecture and conduct workshops abroad, and found this challenging and rewarding (Kaslow, 1990). My awareness of the importance of respect for diversity mounted, and I realized it was essential to become knowledgeable about cultural values regarding marriage and the family, gender issues, parenting, sexuality, handling finances, and the overall socioeconomic context of each region (Comas-Diaz, 1996; N. Kaslow, Celano, & Dreelin, 1995). I indicated that in the past decade I had taught and led workshops in Czechoslovakia, Hungary, Poland, and Russia, and had a particular interest in Eastern Europe because that is where both my maternal and paternal families of origin came from. I also related that I had been the first president of the International Family Therapy Association (1987–1990), was a past president of the American Psychological Association's Division of Family Psychology (1987), and president of the Division of Media Psychology (1993).

Based on our exploratory conversations, Dr. Kelner and I both thought we could work together well, and so launched into taping our program series in August 1993. (Dr. Kelner also contracted with Marsha Bendavid, a special education teacher, to do some more specifically education-focused programs for the series—originally entitled *Parenting Corner*, or *Parenting Survival Kit* in some countries, and her segments were sometimes interspersed with mine during the first two years of the program's existence.)

Selecting the Topics for an International Market

We began by brainstorming to compose a list of topics that we thought would be of interest to our target market. It was not difficult to agree on some high priority issues to launch the series. As we moved along, we kept adding topics to the list periodically. Ideas have been solicited from other members of the VOA program and administrative staff, from colleagues we each know who are interested in such issues, and from visitors to VOA from various countries of the former Soviet Union (more on this later). We continue to be able to generate meaningful topics quite easily.

Shortly after the first few tapes were done, Dr. Kelner was informed that the program was being aired in major Russian cities during "drive time" (peak traffic hour) when people are commuting to or from work. It is an excellent time slot, and many programs are played repeatedly. We also were told that numerous other VOA services and countries were intrigued by the series and had decided to use the tapes. This included, among others, all of Eastern Europe (some in translation), Western Europe (in English), China, Iran, the Central Asia Division, and Burma. Thus, although the target audience remains Russia, we try to make the programs relevant to a very diverse multicultural listening audience—a difficult task when the subject matter revolves around such topics as teenage sexuality, which may not be considered appropriate for discussion in some regions, such as the various Arab countries. We attempt to be tactful without watering down the substance of the program, and realize any country may decide not to use a specific program if it presents too much of a discrepancy of ideas in contrast to their values.

A partial list of the program topics selected and used from August 1993 through fall 1995 appears in the Appendix at the end of this chapter. A wide range of subjects has been covered so that we can impact on the multifaceted needs of a gigantic, extremely heterogeneous listening audience. Themes that have cut across many programs include the importance of listening to one another, the importance of incorporating each others' ideas when possible in a problem solving orientation and process, and the value of using family conferences as a planned time to discuss issues of mutual concern.

An unexpected source of feedback has been the engineers and other personnel at the recording studio at VOA headquarters in Washington, DC. They have often become immersed in the content of the show and have asked Dr. Kelner questions afterwards—a behavior that is quite atypical for them. In addition, when copies of the tapes are left at a centrally designated spot, they and other members of the Washington-based VOA staff take them home to share with spouses, children, and grandchildren. Their comments have been both laudatory and helpful.

In late 1994, a group of journalists and other media people from many states in the eastern regions of the former Soviet Union, like Siberia, visited VOA headquarters in Washington, DC. When they heard about the series, their interest was sparked and they ordered some of the tapes. In addition, they discussed some of the dilemmas that have arisen in their countries as a result of rapid and chaotic economic, political, and social transformations. They requested that we do some programs focusing on such topics as

- Giving children allowance—what it represents.
- Teaching children how to handle money.
- Teaching children to understand financial pressures, crises, and responsibilities.
- Deciding when children work, and who gets what part of their earnings.

These requests were soon fulfilled. Incidents and conversations such as these have constituted another source of ideas for program content.

Breaking News Affects Program Thrust

Selection of program themes is also influenced by prominent news stories of the day. For example, during the time the show has been underway, the war in Bosnia and Croatia has escalated. There have been outbreaks of armed conflict in Angola, South Africa, parts of the Arab world, Israel, Ireland, and elsewhere. Given the mammoth target audience in Eastern Europe, with its proximity to the former country of Yugoslovia, the war there impacts directly on many of their lives. Many who could have fled into neighboring countries. Fears that the kind of prejudice that undergirds holocausts, motivated by a desire for ethnic cleansing, have spread (Charny, 1982). Children see news clippings about the violence and destruction on television. Some have seen it firsthand on the streets where they lived (Kaslow, 1995). Thus we did several segments on such topics as

- Abandoned children. What can society do?
- Dealing with crises and emergencies in families.

- How to talk to children about man-made disasters.
- Impact of war trauma on children.

The explosion internationally of the epidemic of HIV infections and AIDS propelled us to do a program about teenage sexuality and "safer" sex as it relates to the possibility of contracting any sexually transmitted disease (STD). Despite the fact that many of the third world countries showcase displays about AIDS on huge outdoor billboards, the subject still may be conversationally taboo. Thus this program was not used in Iran and some of the other countries that usually air our segments.

Preparing for Each Program

Each time we do a program, we select the topic for the next taping from our existing list, or choose something that is *au courant* that makes an unlisted new subject take priority. Several days before each session, I make a skeleton outline of the four or five major points that seem most important to cover. Since each program can run only five minutes, it is essential to clearly explain the main points. Usually I plan to utilize the first half of the session to talk about either contributory factors or relationship dynamics and perhaps cite a few statistics, and the second half to highlight how to handle the situation or conflict more effectively, by offering several options. If I find I do not know all of the material needed based on many years of reading, teaching, and clinical experience, then I will peruse several resources on the subject and incorporate the most salient facts. Right before taping time, I review my sketchy outline and decide if anything needs to be added or rearranged.

At her end, Dr. Kelner jots down points she wants mentioned and questions she may ask if I do not cover what she has in her agenda based on what she thinks our audience will find most interesting and valuable. We found during the first few programs that they sound best when we leave room for spontaneity in the monologue or dialogue. Therefore, the format has a fireside chat flavor rather than a didactic lecture approach.

Taping Each Segment

Dr. Kelner calls me from her office each week at a designated time. Once we touch base and are sure we are both set to go, we cut the connection and she goes to the studio. As soon as a recording booth and an engineer are available, she calls again. We do a sound check and when we are certain we can hear each other, the taping begins.

As the program host, Dr. Kelner opens each show with a variation of the following: "This is Dr. Kelner. We continue our series on parenting (now family issues; see below for change to expanded focus) with our expert-consultant, family psychologist, Dr. Florence Kaslow. Dr. Kaslow is a former president of the International Family Therapy Association. Today our topic is "_____". At that point I begin to speak, and keep talking in a candid, professional yet chatty manner until and unless Dr. Kelner interjects. Sometimes I speak the entire time until either the clock in front of me or Dr. Kelner indicates that "time is almost up." She then asks for any final summary comments, or she paraphrases one or two points that I have made which she considers most important or likely to be quite new for her listeners.

When the taping is over, we comment on how it went and debrief each other. Sometimes something I've said sparks an idea for another program on a related topic. For example, in early 1996 we discussed spouse abuse. I mentioned that children witnessing violence between their parents are deeply distressed and worried by such behavior. At the conclusion of the taping, Dr. Kelner suggested we do a separate program on "What to do with children who have seen one parent physically abuse the other." This is one of those topics that simply is not talked about in Eastern Europe, the Arab countries, and some other parts of the globe.

In August 1995, Dr. Kelner joined me at the American Psychological Association annual meeting in New York to offer a program under the auspices of the Committee on International Relations in Psychology (CIRP). According to Joan Buchanan, Director of the APA Office of International Affairs, this was the first time VOA was ever officially represented at APA, and we appreciated that Dr. Kelner was given time off from her regular work schedule to come to APA and present. Our tandem presentation was titled, *The Voice of America Around The World*. After the APA meeting, in a letter to VOA Director Geoffrey Cowan thanking him for enabling Dr. Kelner's participation, Ms. Buchanan wrote, "Dr. Kelner's presentation underlined for psychologists the important role that the VOA plays in disseminating worldwide information about such issues as the psychological aspects of parenting" (personal correspondence, August 23, 1995).

Our collaborative efforts continue to bring psychological topics to the attention of VOA program staff, administration, and listeners, who make up a huge new audience for psychological themes, research, and services. In recognition of this, in September 1995, I was invited to a special ceremony by the U.S. Information Agency Bureau of Broadcasting and presented with a Certificate of Appreciation by VOA Director Geoffrey Cowan. The plaque reads, "In recognition of your expert contribution to the success of the VOA Russian language program 'Parenting.' Your selfless and enthusiastic dedication has enabled an idea to grow into a vital link to concerned parents in Russia and neighboring states." Dr. Kelner's recognition of the need, and her presentation of an idea whose time had come, has provided a wonderful opportunity to present psychology through the medium of radio in a most ethical and professional manner in a new forum for discourse.

Phase II—The American Family

In late 1995 some changes in staffing and programming were made at VOA. In the shuffle, our purview was expanded so that the program is now entitled *The American Family*. It is based on the premise that the listening audience is interested in the dilemmas of the American family and how we solve them. By hearing about this, it is hypothesized that listeners will be able to generalize and apply the information to their own lives.

We still give ample attention to the issues of children within the larger family system, as well as to couples' concerns and extended family dilemmas. Some of the topics presented in phase II of this program have been:

- Battered wife syndrome.
- Caring for elderly parents.
- Coping with death of a child, sibling, or beloved grandparent.
- Coping with death of a parent.
- Dealing with elderly parents.
- Differences in ideas about child rearing.
- Disagreements over money.
- In-law problems.
- Issues for dual career couples.
- Techniques for resolving conflicts.
- Tips for a long term, good marriage.
- What to do when one partner is having an affair.
- When parents disagree on child rearing.

Conclusion

Programs such as *Parenting Corner* and *The American Family* provide superb vehicles within which media psychologists can share their professional knowledge, experience, and wisdom about the important area of intrafamilial relationships. We can expound on our concepts, using a combined clinical and research base for the facts and opinions we convey, succinctly differentiating between the two. We can speak ethically about how to improve something, by suggesting options and alternatives in generic terms rather than by giving specific advice (APA, 1994).

Furthermore, presenting to an international audience will challenge media psychologists to continually broaden their grasp of multicultural perspectives and issues (Koss-Chionino & Canive, 1996). In addition, being on international radio, with and through a U.S. governmental agency that represents America's voice to the world, and which, at the most basic and loftiest philosophic level, shares the humanitarian goals and values promulgated by our profession, is a gratifying experience that also enables us to express an aspect of our own patriotism and concern for more peaceful interpersonal and world relationships.

REFERENCES

American Psychological Association. (1994). *Ethical principles of psychologists and code of conduct*. Washington, DC: Author.

Bureau of Broadcasting. (1993). *Looking toward tomorrow*. Washington, DC: USIA.

Charney, I. W. (1982). *How can we commit the unthinkable? Genocide: The human cancer*. Boulder, CO: Westview Press.

Comas-Diaz, L. (1996). Cultural considerations in diagnosis and treatment. In F. W. Kaslow (Ed.), *Handbook of relational diagnosis and dysfunctional family patterns* (pp. 152–168). New York: Wiley.

Kaslow, F. W. (1990). A multifaceted family psychology potpourri. In F. W. Kaslow (Ed.), *Voices in family psychology* (Vol. I, pp. 281–322). Newbury Park, CA: Sage.

Kaslow, F. W. (1995). Nobody's children or everybody's children. In W. J. O'Neill, Jr. (Ed.), *Family: The first imperative* (pp. 165–178). Cleveland: William J. & Dorothy K. O'Neill Foundation.

Kaslow, N. J., Celano, M., & Dreelin, E. F. (1995). A cultural perspective on family theory and therapy. *The Psychiatric Clinics of North America, 18*(3), 621–633.

Koss-Chionino, J. D., & Canive, J. M. (1996). Cultural considerations in diagnosis. In F. W. Kaslow (Ed.), *The handbook of relational diagnosis and dysfunctional family patterns* (pp. 152–170). New York: Wiley.

United States Information Agency. (1995, Spring/Summer). *In the news.* Washington, DC: Office of External Affairs.

Voice of America. (1995, January). *News and information for a global audience.* Washington, DC: Office of External Affairs.

Appendix

Partial Listing of Program Topics Presented on *The Parenting Corner* (1993–1995)

- Adoption: Should parents tell the child about it?
- Boundary issues.
- Changing roles of mothers in families—balancing career and marriage and motherhood.
- Children and poverty.
- Children with ADD and ADHD.
- Children and "bad" company.
- Children and punishment.
- Concerns of adolescent boys and girls.
- Coping with lack of respect.
- Dealing with school failure.
- Discipline and setting limits in the family.
- Divorce: Part 1, How to comfort your children; Part 2, Visitation schedules and issues; Part 3, What should children do when parents start to date?; Part 4, Stepfamilies.
- Encouraging creativity in children.
- Encouraging children to think independently.
- Families in crisis.
- Fathers and daughters.
- Feelings just are: They are neither good nor bad.
- Gifted and talented kids.
- Grandparents and the extended family
- Handling disobedience and rebelliousness.
- Helping children to build self-confidence.
- Helping children to cope with peer pressure.
- Helping children to cope with rape and molestation.
- Helping children to deal with anger.
- Helping children to deal with death of a parent.
- Helping children to learn family values.

- Helping children adapt when they change schools.
- Helping the seriously ill child.
- How parents should react to different styles of their children in manners and music.
- Leaving home: Helping adolescents separate.
- Mothers and sons.
- Motivating achievement in adolescents.
- New roles for fathers.
- Overweight children.
- Parents' past: Should children be told about it?
- Prejudice and how to deal with it.
- Privacy—alone time and space.
- Religion and spirituality.
- Special dilemmas of working mothers.
- Substance abuse.
- Teaching children how to deal with crime and violence.
- Teaching children moral values.
- Teenage sex and the risk of AIDS and pregnancy.
- Teenage love and infatuation.
- When children have parties.
- When and how children manipulate parents.
- When parents are wrong: Should they say so to the children?
- Working mothers—helping them juggle and cope.

The Media Psychologist on TV

Richard Tanenbaum

Telecommunications technology is making television an ever more viable medium with which to educate and inform. Households across the nation now have less expensive means to access a myriad of channels and programming. Communities nationwide are providing opportunities for individuals to present their own programs and points of view on cable access channels. Program distribution and viewership are increasing dramatically.

With the advent of larger television audiences, and the public's interest in gaining understanding about their own experiences and behavior, the role of the TV psychologist is becoming even more formidable. Within the framework of ethical principles and professional guidelines and standards, the media psychologist's mission is to provide the public with useful information. This is a wonderful, yet formidable, task.

This chapter is from the perspective of a practicing TV psychologist who has served as an executive producer and host of children's and health-related television programming. First, I will share my personal journey. Then I will focus on guidelines and tips gleaned over the course of that journey for psychologists who are entering the realm of television.

From Child Psychologist
to Executive Producer/TV Host: One Journey

About six years ago I was in private practice full-time, seeing primarily children and their parents in therapy. I found myself addressing the serious struggles that many children and families face, problems that require professional attention and particular expertise: separation and divorce, academic difficulties, behavior problems in school and at home, depression, fears, and phobias. Many of the difficulties I helped my younger clients work through were interpersonal and social problems like getting teased in school, feeling unpopular and rejected, incompetent or stupid, or uncoordinated and clumsy. Often issues centered around sibling rivalry or feeling pressured to perform optimally in school—both academically and relative to extracurricular activities. These themes surfaced often and had a profound impact on self-esteem, peer relationships, and family interactions.

Although my patients were able to recognize the importance of getting input from a well-trained psychologist, I could not help but think that many of these problems could have been prevented before they became serious enough to warrant professional attention.

As I sat in my office one day, I pondered my desire to teach children how to cope with everyday problems. My goal was to arm them with a repertoire of coping strategies and, ultimately, to prevent more serious difficulties from arising. How could I accomplish this objective most effectively?

Despite the criticism hurled at the television industry, I believed television could be an extraordinarily effective teaching mechanism if used properly. Moreover, if people were lobbying for high quality children's television programming, why not produce a show that addressed children's social and emotional needs? Why not help kids learn how to handle conflict—both in terms of their own notions of self and in regard to their interactions with their world? Maybe such a

program would indeed prevent more serious problems from developing down the road.

So how could something like this work? What kind of a "hook"
would get kids interested in watching? And how would I sell television
industry officials the idea? The answer was simple—make it fun! Use
entertainment to get the message out there.

After the concept began to gel, a myriad of issues needed to be analyzed. In terms of market research, I began to check the networks and
cable stations to find out if a show like this was already being done.
Parents, teachers, and children were asked if they knew of any similar
programming. Surprisingly, the concept appeared rather unique.
Educational TV had not really moved from dealing with the "three R's"
and more academically based topics, to issues surrounding social and
emotional development. It appeared that no existing program focused
on teaching children coping strategies for life.

Next, the target audience needed to be determined. A preponderance
of children's television was geared to preschool children. Interestingly,
there was hardly any programming for preteens, children 9 to 12 years of
age. This seemed like an appropriate age group to focus on. To learn more
about educating this particular age group, I consulted with an educator.

I also interviewed over 50 children about the kind of shows they
liked to watch. The majority of these kids preferred programs that were
fast-paced and entertaining. In addition, they liked shows that featured
other children their age or older. Taking into account the information
from my educator colleague, I began to think about specific methods
with which to disseminate information and how to draw upon my
training as a psychologist.

Fortunately, I also had experience as an entertainer to draw upon. A
very vivid and fond recollection is awakening one morning at about 4 a.m.
(much, much earlier than usual for me—I'm a night person!) and knowing,
without a doubt, how I could combine my various skills. I bolted out of
bed, ran into the living room, finished a bag of Oreos, and began what was
for all intents and purposes a "one man show." With my creative juices
flowing, I created five characters I could portray. Through these characters
or personalities, information—psychological in nature—would be delivered to children in an entertaining and hopefully effective fashion.

What seemed like a good idea turned out to be the selling point for
the show. About a month before I came up with the plan to create a
cadre of characters, I had the good fortune to meet a relatively well-
known television producer in New York. I had pitched the original

show idea to him, hoping to garner his support and assistance. He thought it was a terrific notion and was especially intrigued with the fact that I was a psychologist and a trained actor. In his opinion, my professional credentials added a great deal to the credibility and worthiness of the project.

I produced a very rough (at the time I thought it was superb) demo tape for him to view. Basically, it featured eight children sitting in a circle with me discussing a variety of issues that were important to them. I left the tape with him and was waiting for his feedback when the idea about using characters, instead of myself, surfaced. Very excited, I called him and told him about my burgeoning alter egos. After some hesitation, he asked me to prepare and forward him another tape that featured the characters.

The characters were forced to come to life in record time. So Ricky the Rock Star, Dr. T. N. Crumpet, Pops, Tex, Dr. Cosa, and Madeline took form quickly. I arranged to have another demo tape produced. Titled *Ask Dr. T.,* it featured a question and answer session between several children and the various characters. I received a call from the producer after he had viewed both tapes. Trying to be as diplomatic as possible, he said, "We loved the characters, but we didn't like Dr. T." My first thought was thank goodness for the characters! In all seriousness, his feedback was of exceptional importance. He went on to explain that Dr. T. appeared rather stiff and overly academic. In his opinion, the characters were much less threatening and much more entertaining. It was a "go" for the characters.

A small team of professionals was then put together to best market the project. In addition to the educational specialist, I also consulted with public relations and marketing specialists to develop appropriate print materials and fact sheets to use when trying to sell the concept. My New York producer contact also agreed to talk to his colleagues about the project and elicit their support and assistance. A cascade of contacts and potential leads began flowing. I did my best to be open to every possibility and follow every lead to its conclusion.

A Jones Intercable, Inc. affiliate in the Washington, DC area invited me to appear on a talk show they were doing to discuss children's issues and also to describe my program's concept. I told the host of that show that I would like to "bring" the characters on with me and have them air their thoughts about kids and how to help them cope. She agreed!

This was probably the most significant turning point in the project. The talk show was a great success. The host interviewed me as well as three of the characters. Two days after taping the talk show, Jones Intercable, Inc. agreed to produce the *Dr. T. and Company* series! With their support and competent production staff, we created the first version of the show. It was ultimately seen in over 10 states, was offered free to other stations around the country as a public service, and ran weekly for 3 years.

Now that we had a good demo tape (we used pieces of actual shows), it was time to do an "all out" marketing campaign while the show was still running. Armed with a revised press kit that included articles written about the show, I traveled to New York and Los Angeles on a frequent basis, trying to push the show to the next level. This experience was humbling, to say the least!

I was fortunate to have the opportunity to meet with children's television officials from ABC, CBS, NBC, and Fox. Despite the success of the show, focus group results indicating interest and enthusiasm on the part of parents and children, and the advent of the Children's Television Act requiring broadcasters to air educational programming, the networks were not interested in taking the "risk" of producing the show on a larger scale.

They believed that children were more interested in watching animated programs (cartoons) than live-action shows, and that 9- to 12-year-olds were a hard audience to reach; they were busy doing other things. In addition, they were not convinced that a program dealing with mental health issues could really be entertaining enough to keep children watching. I learned that many of these people, however, shared my altruism and my wish to do something meaningful and beneficial for children.

Networks and cable companies, like all businesses, are concerned about the "bottom line." I was informed that if a corporate sponsor or grant moneys could be found, they would consider producing the program. All the executives I met with invited me to keep them informed of my progress and were open to providing ongoing guidance and suggestions.

Somewhat disheartened, I continued attempting to find the next home for *Dr. T. and Company*. We produced a new, "broadcast quality" demo tape and continued our marketing efforts. Interestingly, about a month after finishing this demo, I was contacted by NET (National Empowerment Television), a new national satellite network. The general manager's children had been watching *Dr. T. and Company* on a local cable station and loved it! NET had just hired an Emmy-award-winning producer to direct their children's television division and was very interested in producing the next version of the program.

After much negotiation and legal work, we collaborated on the project. I hosted the show and served as executive producer. Owning the rights to the program, I was also given the option of selling the fully produced episodes of the program to other television entities. We changed the format of the show, added original music and an ample studio audience, and established an 800 number for children, parents, and teachers to comment about the program, ask questions, or suggest topics for future shows.

Creating as interactive a program as possible, children and schools from around the country sent in video spots about the "topic of the day" that were integrated into the various episodes. In addition, the characters now made only cameo appearances and were no longer an integral part of the program. We worked on making "Dr. T." an interesting, exciting, and entertaining TV host.

Dr. T. Productions, Inc., in association with NET, produced this version of the program until December 1995. At that time, NET decided to concentrate on political programming only. After enjoying great success (the show was available in over four million homes across the country), *Dr. T. and Company* was discontinued. At present, we are still pursuing a new home for the show. In addition, we are considering packaging the show as an educational video series for home or school use.

Innovative television programming can provide children with coping strategies for managing challenging situations. I remember one mother telling us that her son's social anxiety moderated to such a significant extent after participating on *Dr. T. and Company* that he was later able to audition and get the role of the Little Drummer Boy in the school Christmas play. Many other parents and children wrote to us thanking us for helping them in some way or another. The show seemed to be accomplishing its objectives.

In my long journey with *Dr. T. and Company* I learned much about being a media psychologist on TV. The next section of the chapter presents some of the tips, lessons, and guidelines gleaned along the way.

General Guidelines and Tips

Tips for Promoting a Television Program Concept

- Be aggressive but not obnoxious!
- Respect the expertise of the people you are dealing with.
- Take off your clinical/academic hat when necessary.
- Speak the language of the audience you are addressing.

- Follow every lead to its conclusion.
- Tell everybody what you are doing. It's a small world and people know people who can help.
- Learn how to handle rejection and persevere. Don't take "no" for an answer.
- Use criticism constructively. Listen to what people are saying.
- Get used to making cold calls. If the idea's well thought out and good, people will listen.
- Keep in touch with everyone you have contacted. A postcard will suffice.
- Make sure you're putting your best foot forward. Sometimes you have only one chance.
- Involve others. Don't assume that you are an expert about everything!
- Learn the industry!
- Hire an entertainment attorney to help you through negotiations and to protect your work.
- Consider using a publicist who can help you package and market your idea.
- Make sure it is an endeavor that you enjoy! The project can come to a screeching halt if you're not having fun!

Other Television Situations

In addition to educational TV shows, there is an interesting assortment of television situations in which a media psychologist may participate. Psychologists often appear on news broadcasts and in documentaries. Some news channels are even beginning to use psychologists to provide regular commentary on subjects like parenting, depression, or phobias. Daytime and prime-time magazine programs often feature psychologist guests to discuss newsworthy topics or new books they have written.

The television talk show is by far the most common forum for the TV psychologist. Ricki Lake, Jenny Jones, Sally, and Oprah—to name just a few—are not unfamiliar names to us. It is no news that this format is extremely popular, and it seems as though each day brings a new television talk show with a supposedly novel slant.

Some daytime "talks" do an adequate job of presenting psychologist guests in a good light and featuring circumstances and situations that we all may face at one time or another. Some even offer helpful advice. However, it is not uncommon for some tabloids and talk shows to trivialize mental health issues and exploit individuals.

Many focus and elaborate on rather extreme examples of familial discord and interpersonal conflict. Well choreographed, such topics elicit strong emotional reactions among the studio audience, "guests," hosts, and viewers. The media psychologist should guard against participating in shows which are exhibitionist rather than educational. Harm can be done to both the participants and the viewers by such shows.

Role of the Media Psychologist on TV

Regardless of the particular television situation, the media psychologist must be clear about his or her role. When defining one's role in regard to a media event, the TV psychologist should consider the extent to which he or she is functioning as a

- resource specialist,
- educator, or
- facilitator.

Resource Specialist

When serving as a resource, the psychologist must remain keenly aware of appropriate language for the audience being addressed. This involves particular vocabulary and minimizing the use of jargon. Although detail may help people understand the concepts being conveyed, concentrating on fine points at the expense of broader issues may confuse or alienate an audience. Although we may be passionate about "the literature," our listeners are not always interested in particular research findings or theoretical concepts. People want information and solutions; they want strategies they can apply to specific life situations. Being clear, concise, and focused at all times is an important rule of thumb.

Given our credentials, "talking down" to our audience is an all too common pitfall. Talk show panelists and audiences tune out when they feel they are being devalued, labeled, or categorized. Using language (verbal and nonverbal), inflection, and tone to communicate parity and respect are powerful tools that foster trust. This sets the stage for people to open up to thinking in a different way or trying something new. Appropriate self-disclosure also assists in helping one's audience see you as authentic, or someone who understands, and as a person with whom they can relate.

Educator

Beyond our role as resource specialist, we are required to educate our audiences. As discussed above, the language we use and the style of our presentation are important factors. To communicate most effectively, however, we need to have a working knowledge of educational principles. Most importantly, we must be well acquainted with the topic we are addressing, and have developed techniques to communicate technical and theoretical information in a way our listeners can understand.

It is helpful to have a mental outline of what you hope to accomplish. Similar to preparing a lecture or lesson plan, thinking about your presentation in terms of a beginning, middle, and end provides an appropriate structure that keeps you on task. For example, laying the groundwork in an introductory statement primes an audience, letting them know what they can expect. A summary or closing statement reinforces important points you have addressed. Using this technique also assists you in managing your own anxiety, especially when you have to deal with the unexpected!

Another important strategy is determining key points to highlight before a particular media event. To do this most effectively, it is useful to know the demographics of a particular audience. Finally, be careful not to overwhelm your viewers with too many helpful hints, things to do, books to read, or organizations to call.

Facilitator

One of the most challenging roles of the TV psychologist is to facilitate discussions and interactions on television talk shows. This involves attending to comments from the studio audience, the show's host, and the panelists or guests, who are usually struggling with a significant relational problem or conflict. In many instances, the psychologist has not previously met these individuals and has only a very circumscribed knowledge of their personalities, their lives, and their particular difficulties. In some cases, the panelists and psychologist have only a cursory meeting at best in the green room prior to going on the show.

Given the fact that the television studio is by no means a consultation room, the media psychologist is required to adapt to a myriad of influences and adopt a style that is appropriate, effective, and ethical. Although tempting, we need to be very cautious about offering specific advice or solutions to people with whom we are not acquainted. Another reason to refrain is that the panelists or guests may not be ready to listen to, or integrate, suggestions about how to begin resolving their problems.

As facilitator, our objectives must be realistic. It may be reasonable to listen attentively, reflect what an individual is feeling and thinking, and offer an empathic response. It may also be appropriate to identify coping strategies, as long as such recommendations will by no means jeopardize the individual's well-being and safety. Suggesting that a generic solution is appropriate for all people who are dealing with similar difficulties is unethical and inaccurate. However, specific therapeutic suggestions are also not appropriate and must be generalized somewhat. Moreover, one cannot assume that an individual has an accurate understanding of the information being provided, or is capable of successfully incorporating a particular suggestion.

It is also imperative that the media psychologist maintain boundaries and set limits. Although yelling, shouting, and other forms of acting out may yield high ratings, it is important for the psychologist to take active steps to diffuse a volatile situation when necessary. Our task is not to treat these individuals or engage in any type of therapeutic alliance. Instead, providing information about organizations or facilities that may be able to offer assistance should be an overriding objective.

Training Considerations for the Media Psychologist on TV

Graduate school programs do not train us to work with the media. Although it may look simple, talking to the camera and getting your point across to a television audience are not easy tasks. Besides a good dose of encouragement and support from friends and family, interacting effectively with reporters, journalists, and television personnel also requires specific skills and specialized instruction. To perform at our best, it is necessary to supplement our training.

Verbal Behavior and Vocal Techniques

Attending professional meetings will convince anyone that we are not all born with presentation skills. It is a challenge to keep an audience interested and to communicate ideas effectively. Our voice and how we use it is critical to the success or failure of a presentation.

First, one must be heard. Some people find it hard to establish and maintain an appropriate volume. Still others may need to engage in voice-building exercises to develop the capacity for greater volume. Voice building involves physical and vocal exercises and may require the assistance of a voice coach. Recording yourself reading aloud allows you to monitor your presentation style and target problem areas and correct them.

Second, the TV psychologist needs to be aware of tone. Tone is defined by the pitch, quality, and richness of the voice. Oftentimes, the more pleasing the voice, the greater the audience's attention. A voice that is shrill or too "muddy" can be unpleasant to the ear. To some degree, we can moderate this characteristic. Adjusting vocal tone involves learning how to "open" and "place" the voice by exercising and controlling certain musculature. As with vocal volume, breathing exercises that ultimately provide "support" for the voice are also involved in moderating vocal tone (personal communication with Elizabeth Vrenios, director of the Music Department, American University, Washington, DC). Once again, instruction from a voice coach may be helpful.

The third component of vocal technique is diction. Diction refers to the clarity with which words are pronounced. The rate at which we speak is another important element of diction. Individuals who are not using their first language often have significant diction problems. Also, those who have strong regional accents or who do not have much experience with public speaking may need to visit a speech therapist or voice coach to improve their diction. Good diction is central to a successful presentation.

Inflection is the fourth variable to address. For the most part, inflection has to do with incorporating versatility into your voice. Most of us are comfortable with raising the tone or pitch of our voice at the end of a question or modulating our voices when talking to a child, partner, or spouse. It is easy to lose an audience if we are not conscious of our inflection. If we speak in a monotone, that is, with uniform, static inflection, regardless of the content, what we say may come across as uninteresting to the listener. We have all seen people nod off at meetings. Regardless of the subject matter, changing and altering inflection can have a powerful effect on keeping your audience awake and interested. As with other aspects of vocal technique, inflection is a skill that must be practiced. The reader is referred to Brown's (1989) excellent book, *Your Public Best*, for a comprehensive discussion of presenting on television.

Nonverbal Behavior

Nonverbal behavior is another significant factor to consider when appearing on television. Specifically, the media psychologist has to get used to addressing the camera. The camera, after all, is representative of your largest audience. The unnatural aspect of looking into a lens and not seeing anyone or having any feedback makes this a none-too-easy task. The need to address as many as three cameras adds to the challenge of this situation.

The only way to become comfortable on camera is to practice. Rehearsing with a camcorder is very helpful. What's especially useful is to assemble a group of people and videotape a presentation. Practice shifting your attention from the live audience to the camera until you are comfortable. When you watch the tape, pay close attention to the subtle and obvious differences in your appearance and manner when talking to the camera.

Mannerisms are another aspect of nonverbal behavior. All of us have developed particular unconscious behaviors over time. Many of these mannerisms are manifested when addressing another individual or a group of persons. Some of us may roll our eyes when we are annoyed or exasperated. Others might have a tendency to fold their arms and avert their gaze when addressing certain people or discussing particular topics. Even more subtle are behaviors like pulling our ears, scratching, or biting our nails.

To be successful we need to become conscious of these unconscious pieces of behavior. Uncontrolled mannerisms can distract an audience and contradict or confuse the messages we are trying to relate. Fortunately, a prolonged psychoanalysis that explores intrapsychic issues related to these phenomena is, for most of us, unnecessary. Once again, the use of a camcorder provides a more affordable and efficient solution to this problem. In addition, asking for feedback from friends and colleagues, although it is sometimes embarrassing, can help us identify our idiosyncratic quirks.

A few specific nonverbal behaviors should be mentioned. Good eye contact is an essential ingredient in television work. Whether you are looking at your studio audience, addressing your television audience through the camera, or interacting with the panelists, direct eye-contact adds power and intensity to your statements. Smiling or even laughing when appropriate can relax your listeners, and helps people view you as in touch and genuine. Image considerations are important, and coming across as too clinical or academic is not always advantageous.

Good posture and an open physical style are also useful in keeping the audience attentive. Sitting closer to the edge of your chair and leaning forward when addressing people can give you an advantage when appearing on television. What's most important is to become keenly aware of the nuances of your behavior and how it impacts others. With awareness comes control. Like great entertainers, being able to pick and choose behaviors from an endless array of techniques and strategies— verbal and nonverbal—affords us versatility, flexibility, and the capacity to "work" almost any audience.

Appearance

As important as nonverbal and verbal style is appearance. Entertainment industry officials will tell you to always look your best. Our first response might be to dismiss this advice as obvious and not deserving of much energy or thought. That would be a big mistake. Although sometimes hard to admit, appearance has a strong effect on our image and how we are perceived by others. Wardrobe, make-up, and hairstyle are salient aspects of our appearance and are important to emphasize.

Looking your best is more complex than you might first imagine. Adopting a set style that is unchanging is not always beneficial. Although it is important to feel comfortable, adapting our "look" to a variety of situations is also necessary. Knowing our audience and the kind of image we want to portray can help us hone in on a particular ensemble style. For example, what may be right for one talk show is not necessarily correct for another. A psychologist providing commentary on a news program may need to adjust his or her wardrobe for an appearance on a documentary or a morning magazine program. Although our friends, family, and peers may give us useful feedback, discussing these issues with other media psychologists, television people, and fashion/makeup consultants is usually much more helpful.

There are several training resources for the media psychologist on TV. As mentioned previously, a vocal coach and speech therapist can provide significant assistance. Division 46 (Media Psychology) of the American Psychological Association (APA) also sponsors training seminars for media psychologists. These are invaluable workshops that are offered every year at the annual APA convention. Some state associations also provide similar training opportunities. Joining Division 46 is a must for any psychologist interested in pursuing television or radio work.

AFTRA (American Federation of Television and Radio Artists) and SAG (The Screen Actors Guild) offer a myriad of conservatory courses to union members. On-Camera Training, TV News, Centering Techniques, and Make-Up for Film and Video, are a sample of some of the workshops offered (personal communication with AFTRA regional office, Chevy Chase, MD.) Whether or not you choose to participate in the conservatory, I strongly recommend joining AFTRA. Membership puts you in touch with people in the television and radio field. It is a good source of contacts and affords wonderful opportunities for networking.

Preparing for an Appearance

Getting the Call

You get a call and are offered a job. What do you do? First, determine if you're the right person for the job. As much as you may love to do this type of work, if you are not an expert in the subject or do not have time to familiarize yourself with important details, you may want to suggest a colleague who may be more appropriate. Assuming that you are going to pursue this opportunity, you must ask a series of questions to make sure you understand what you are being asked to do.

The "who, what, where, when, and how" method is very effective in getting crucial questions answered. As alluded to throughout this chapter, it is essential to know your audience. It is also important to know if you will be offering only commentary or interacting with people. Specifically, does the producer view you primarily as a *resource*, or as a *facilitator*, someone who will actively engage with guests and a studio audience?

Having this conversation also allows you to clear up any ethical concerns immediately. If you feel that you are being asked to participate in a manner that is inappropriate or unethical, you must say no. If reasonable, delineate conditions for your participation. For example, suppose you were guesting on a show dealing with panic disorder. You may want to require the producer to agree to provide names and phone numbers of organizations that can offer assistance and support. In addition, it may be necessary to establish the importance of after-care arrangements for talk show participants. Remember, end the conversation with the producer only when you are clear about what is expected of you, and details of your role have been identified and discussed.

Making the Call

We don't always have to wait by the phone for someone to call. Many media psychologists take an active role in following community, national, or world news. When a psychologist can offer the public useful information about a particular event or situation, it is perfectly reasonable to "pitch" an idea to a variety of television or radio producers. Sometimes they'll bite. If nothing else, it is a very good exercise. You get practice making cold calls and learn a great deal about the industry and the various types of people involved.

Ethical Considerations

Finally, it is imperative that the TV psychologist be cognizant of specific ethical considerations. First and foremost, the media psychologist must not diagnose or treat individuals on radio or television. Whether you are interacting one-on-one, addressing a studio audience, or speaking to your television or radio listeners, this is indeed an ethical violation. You may not treat an individual over the airwaves. Professionalism also involves evaluating your competence to serve in a particular fashion. As exciting as television work may be, we need to say no when we are asked to overstep the bounds of our professional expertise or if we are asked to be part of a program we believe will require too much self-disclosure of participants.

Maintaining confidentiality is a primary responsibility of the media psychologist. As a TV psychologist, we often have the opportunity to meet personalities and become immersed in the entertainment world. Such exposure may also put us in touch with celebrities who are requesting assistance. High visibility and the tenacity of the media in encouraging psychologists to express opinions about celebrities' behavior or their personalities can obscure the lines separating what is and what is not ethical behavior. Remaining aware of the unique pressures we may experience, and seeking assistance or consultation when necessary, keeps us on track, clear about our objectives, and certain about the ethical nature of our actions.

There continues to be much discussion about the applicability of ethical guidelines to the practice of media psychology. As for any psychologist, the media psychologist must adhere to the current code of ethics for psychologists, as published by the APA, and the Guidelines for Media Psychologists currently before the APA governance. If questions arise about ethics in regard to particular actions, activities, or situations, the psychologist is encouraged to consult with colleagues and the APA Ethics Office.

Conclusion

As we move into the 21st century, the trend toward personal health management—taking responsibility for one's own mental and physical well-being—continues. As a result, psychology is becoming increasingly important in people's lives. People want to understand the impact of their life experiences and how to cope more effectively with life's stresses. The applicability and relevance of psychological principles continue to increase.

Television remains a powerful communications tool, and is becoming an even more effective teaching medium. TV audiences and viewership are growing. Specialty networks are being launched, and new programming abounds. With these developments come a multitude of opportunities for the media psychologist. Besides appearing on venues such as talk shows, news broadcasts, and magazine programs, psychologists are becoming regular commentators and health reporters. Some are even hosting their own shows. My personal experience in this field has been extremely stimulating and rewarding; and the door is opening wider and wider for any of us who want to be a part of this exciting phenomenon.

These same opportunities bring significant challenges. TV psychologists must work with the television industry and other psychologists to clearly define and establish their role. Strategies for how we might best serve the public also need to be developed. Our continued success hinges on taking advantage of specialty training opportunities and creating new ones.

Maintaining professional standards and integrity, and realizing the limits of our expertise, is of utmost importance. New professional practice opportunities bring with them new issues to resolve, questions and concerns, and moral dilemmas. As our profession continues to evolve, ethical principles need to remain at the heart of how we practice psychology. Television will continue to allow us to reach more and more people and make significant contributions to individuals and to society. The future is brimming with opportunities for us to practice our discipline in creative and effective ways.

REFERENCE

Brown, L. (1989). *Your public best*. New York: Newmarket Press.

New Roles for Psychologists in the Mass Media

Lawrence Kutner

The mass media offer psychologists new and increasing opportunities to exercise their skills, training, and insights. Whether with traditional media such as newspapers and magazines, or with such rapidly expanding resources as cable and satellite television and the World Wide Web, psychologists now have an opportunity to stretch the limits of not only how we practice our profession but of how we view ourselves and our roles.

This chapter will explore some innovative and ethical ways psychologists can become involved in mass communications. Although many of my references are to formal research, much of my commentary

This chapter is based in part on a presentation by Lawrence Kutner, PhD, and Cheryl K. Olson, SD, at the American Association of Family and Consumer Sciences National Research and Policy Agenda on Investment in Youth, Roanoke, VA, June 2–4, 1995.

springs from personal experience. This is, after all, a relatively new and rapidly changing field. Still, these are the views of one nondispassionate participant and observer, and should be treated as such.

I have also taken the liberty of including some autobiographical information. This is not to imply that my professional path is typical or that others should try to replicate it. Rather, my experiences at the interface of psychology and mass communications lend perspective to the conclusions I reached and suggestions I make.

Many academic psychologists and other scientists view the mass media with mixed emotions. Although their social influence may be acknowledged and their political power respected, the newsroom and broadcast studio are *terrae incognitae*. Dealing with reporters, producers, and editors is a task for which researchers and clinicians only rarely receive any training as graduate students. Communicating academic research to the general public is often viewed as vain at best, and potentially unethical at worst.

I shared that disdain when I started graduate school. I trained as a traditional clinical psychologist with a doctorate from a research-oriented program (The University of Minnesota) and clinical training at major medical centers (e.g., the Mayo Clinic). What changed my perception was the experience I had during the summer of 1976, when I was awarded a Mass Media Science Fellowship by the American Association for the Advancement of Science.

That fellowship allowed me to work at the CBS television affiliate in Minneapolis on science- and health-related programming. During part of my time there I coproduced a documentary series on an issue that a correspondent and I felt was a major social issue for the community: juvenile prostitution. (At the time, the Minneapolis–St. Paul area was known as the single largest "exporter" of teenage prostitutes to other cities. Many of the children involved were less than 13 years old. Few people—especially public policy makers—dared to talk about the problem in public.)

Susan Spencer (now a correspondent for CBS News) and I worked for a month on that documentary series. We explored the roots of the problem, examined the lack of services to help these children, and showed how other communities were more successful at handling it.

Airing that series brought the issue to the forefront of public discussion. As a result, state laws regarding pimping were changed, a safe house was started for the young girls, and the matter became an issue in that year's mayoral race in Minneapolis. I also realized that I did more to help those children with a month of work in television than I probably could do in 20 years as a regular clinician.

That experience led me to look at mass media work as an extension of my practice as a clinical psychologist. In fact, I have for the past 20 years thought of myself not as a traditional clinician but as a public health psychologist who uses mass media as an integral tool in my work. This change in orientation has led me to work in a variety of media.

Since leaving traditional psychology, I have worked as the lead journalist for the development of the PBS series *The Brain*, developed a syndicated radio series on science, been a major market and network television reporter and documentary producer covering health and science issues, spent 7 years as a nationally syndicated *New York Times* columnist writing about child development, worked as a columnist and contributing editor to *Parents* magazine, helped develop a new cable television channel focusing on raising young children, written five popular books on child development and parenting, and been a media and psychology consultant to organizations ranging from Microsoft and General Mills to the International Youth Foundation and the Carnegie Corporation of New York. Little in my formal training prepared me for this path.

A Bit of History

Today's psychologists who look for ways to incorporate the mass media into their careers often find that they are stepping onto shaky ground. Will their colleagues perceive them as egotists who thrive on personal publicity or who are looking to promote their own practices? Will they be seen as mere popularizers instead of serious researchers and clinicians? Will they be thought of as charlatans?

It has not helped the image of this aspect of psychology that some of the most popular early media psychologists had questionable credentials or espoused eccentric theories. Perhaps the most famous of these early media psychologists was John B. Watson, the founder of behaviorism. Although his academic credentials were impeccable, his advice to parents was sometimes bizarre. Many introductory psychology texts still quote his suggestions regarding parent–child affection as an example of the tenor of his time—and also perhaps as an object lesson in the dangers of communicating psychological research and theories directly to the public:

> Never hug and kiss them, never let them sit on your lap. If you must, kiss them once on the forehead when they say good night. . . .

> Remember when you are tempted to pet your child that mother love is a dangerous ... instrument which may inflict a never healing wound, a wound which may make infancy unhappy, adolescence a nightmare, an instrument which may wreck your adult son or daughter's vocational future and their chances for marital happiness. (Watson, 1928, pp. 81–87)

Watson was the media guru of American developmental psychology in the early 20th century. He wrote a popular column for *Harper's* magazine, and often gave advice in the then-new *Parents* magazine as well. He was dissatisfied with the ways parents raised their children. Instead, he envisioned a world in which children would be raised on "baby farms" where hundreds of infants could be scientifically observed:

> In his ideal world, child rearing would be brought as much as possible under laboratory control. Mothers would not know the identity of their children. Breast feeding would be prohibited, and children would be rotated among families at four-week intervals until the age of twenty. (Buckley, 1989, p. 163)

Declarations such as Watson's put parents in emotional quicksand. No matter what they did, it was wrong—and it dragged them deeper into an abyss of self-blame and unwarranted guilt. Watson eventually left psychological research to devote all of his time to working with the mass media. He went into the advertising business, and is credited with writing the slogan, "I'd walk a mile for a Camel."

The federal government also got involved in a form of media psychology through the Children's Bureau, a branch of the Department of Labor that was founded in 1912. The Children's Bureau was mandated to "investigate and report ... upon all matters pertaining to the welfare of children and child life among all classes of our people ..." (Tobey, 1925).

In addition to conducting research on such topics as the effects on children of their mothers' employment outside the home during World War I, the Children's Bureau launched an innovative publishing and information dissemination campaign, creating and distributing countless reports, books, and pamphlets with titles ranging from *Save 100,000 Babies, Get a Square Deal for Children* to *Patriotic Play Week: Suggestions to Local Committees*. It also distributed what were known as "dodgers"—short, instructional handbills on basic child-care and child-development topics like "What Do Growing Children Need?" and "Feeding the Child."

Well before parents could write to a nationally syndicated newspaper columnist such as Ann Landers or *Dear Abby* for psychological or child development advice, they could write to the Children's Bureau, which received more than 100,000 such letters each year. Many of that era's government-sanctioned responses reflected business and psychology's fascination with time-and-motion studies. The advice given parents often sounded more like that of an efficiency expert on the floor of a factory than of a developmental psychologist—with predictably dismal results.

Opportunities for Psychologists

Because many of my experiences within the mass media have focused on issues related to developmental psychology and health, I will use those general areas in my examples of how psychologists can use their special skills and training in working with the mass media. You should not feel, however, that psychologists are limited to working in those areas. (Indeed, one of the most interesting experiences I had as a reporter was describing work by some mathematicians that involved structures in four-dimensional hyperspace. What made it particularly challenging was that I was describing this on the radio, so I had no access to visual models to help my audience comprehend what hyperspace is all about!)

One area where psychologists have a clear role is in gaining appropriate public exposure to social intervention programs that are based on psychological or developmental principles, or both. Such exposure is often critical to the long-term success of such programs, for it can lead to awareness not only by the community but also by key public policy makers and legislators.

Deciding on and designing a dissemination strategy can be as complex and painstaking a task as any other portion of a research project. Failing to provide adequate materials or to anticipate possible pitfalls can lead to the mass media and the public ignoring or, worse yet, misinterpreting your findings and recommendations.

I will examine the roles psychologists can play in two approaches to disseminating information: media advocacy and risk reduction communication campaigns. Although those two approaches overlap, the former focuses on conveying information through news stories in established media, whereas the latter focuses on creating and distributing one's own "information products" such as television and radio programs (including commercials and public service announcements), print materials, billboards, and the like. I will also review some of the research on what appear to be critical factors in designing effective communications strategies.

Media Advocacy

At its simplest level, media advocacy involves convincing key representatives of established media outlets, such as newspapers, magazines, and broadcasters, that they should report on the programs or issues in which you are involved. It is a tool for reaching a large number of people efficiently. Unfortunately, many professionals involved in intervention programs do not take advantage of this opportunity. When they do, they frequently do little more than issue a news release or hold a press conference—and wonder why the media apparently have so little interest.

Becoming an advocate for a project or issue through the mass media can require considerable planning, and often calls upon many of the same skills needed by an academic researcher. A first step is to look at the jobs of reporters, producers, and editors from their perspective. By doing so, you will significantly increase the likelihood that the information you wish to present will be covered in a timely and accurate fashion.

There are several guides to help do this, and to help researchers prepare for interviews (Fox and Levin, 1993; Kutner and Olson, 1995). Media training and mock interviews are especially valuable to psychologists who need to learn and practice the specific skills required for being interviewed on radio and television.

It is important to remember not to get swept away in an effort to reach the largest number of people with your message. The target audience for a mass media campaign can be as small as one person: a key legislator or other government official, or the president of a large company. Schwartz (1973, 1983) has given several examples of successful, highly targeted media advocacy and communication campaigns.

Although we use the term "news stories" when describing the content of a newspaper, magazine, or news broadcast, we often gloss over the importance of the two components of the phrase. An awareness of both is critical when trying to convince journalists to cover a story. News contains something new, of course, but it need not be new in the sense that it has only recently happened or been discovered. The newness of information may come from having a different perspective, or an increased relevance to the lives of viewers, listeners, or readers. Similarly, few news organizations cover issues per se. Instead, in a tradition as old as mankind, they tell stories that help us make sense of our lives and the world around us.

Those are the things for which journalists are searching: new information told through a dramatic story, complete with compelling characters and the occasional unexpected plot twist. For example, Wallack and colleagues (1993) tell the story of a family physician in Sacramento, California, who wanted to do something about handgun violence against children. His focus was on children who shot children. Usually these shootings are accidental—often the result of children playing with a real gun as if it were a toy.

Although such shootings are routinely covered as "spot news," little was being done by the media to explore the underlying causes. The first step was to publish an article (Wintemute, Teret, Kraus, Wright, & Bradfield, 1987) in the *Journal of the American Medical Association*, which is routinely received by news organizations. The article used descriptive epidemiology (sometimes called "guerrilla epidemiology" when used this way) to examine the deaths of 88 children under the age of 14 who had been shot by other children in California over a 6-year period. Because of the compelling nature of the topic, the American Medical Association prepared a video news release, which was distributed to television stations and networks throughout the United States to encourage coverage of the research report.

One goal of the authors was to apply pressure for a ban on toy guns that closely resembled real guns. At a news conference timed to coincide with the publication of the paper, the authors made their point by showing a board on which they mounted real guns next to the look-alike toy guns, and challenged the reporters to tell the difference. The coverage gained from this dramatic and highly visual approach allowed the authors to apply enough pressure on Toys R Us, the largest retailer of toy guns in the country, that the store chain discontinued selling the look-alike toys. Other retailers followed suit.

This type of multi-stage advocacy must be carefully planned if it is to be effective. One way of organizing such a plan is through a strategy memo: an internal document of less than a dozen pages that summarizes the issues to be tackled, the anticipated difficulties and sources of support, and the techniques to be used. It is critical that a strategy memo be highly focused, especially when dealing with a large issue that has numerous components. Although lowering the rate of teenage smoking, for example, is a noble goal, it is far too broad a topic for a single media advocacy program. A better approach would be to choose a specific aspect of the problem for each strategy memo.

For example, your goal is to reduce the relatively easy access that children and adolescents have to cigarettes. A strategy memo on that topic might begin with what you believe to be the best way to frame the issue to the public. What are not only the facts but the emotions that can come into play? A strategy memo on teenage smoking might use the following approach:

> Our best bet is to frame the issue as a moral one—the protection of innocent, easily influenced children, especially preteens. This will work for parents and general audiences. With business groups, we can also show that preventing addiction to smoking in children is much easier and cheaper than getting adults to quit later on, thereby reducing health insurance costs.

Next, consider the degree of awareness of the issue, both by the general public and key individuals such as local legislators.

> Since the sale of cigarettes to minors in our state is illegal, most people don't think about the problem, even though those laws are routinely ignored. Surveys indicate that voters think smoking rates have decreased over the past decade more than they really have. They are not aware that teenage smoking rates have stabilized. . . .
>
> We need to raise awareness of the widespread violation of these laws, and the harmful effects this has on children. The recent publicity about the marketing of Camel cigarettes through the use of a cartoon character has elevated the children and smoking issue temporarily, which makes this a good time to act. . . .

Outline the strategies and tactics you will use in presenting this topic both to government officials and to the media.

> Create a climate of concern about children and cigarettes through the use of local media. We can build on the publicity about preschoolers knowing Joe Camel's face as well as Mickey Mouse's (Fischer et al., 1991), perhaps trying a variation of this study with local children to create a "news peg" and good visuals for local TV news. Encourage local newspaper editors to write an editorial about this, noting that the average age for children to start smoking is 13 and that 4000 U.S. children start to smoke each day. . . .
>
> Identify a problem with children's access to and use of cigarettes in the local community. Start by doing a school-based survey of children's smoking prevalence. Compare this with existing national data. If rates are higher than elsewhere, we can appeal to the pressing need for change. . . .

If the community still is not willing to act, try an educational effort consisting of signs, brochures, and other educational materials regarding the law against selling to minors, the need to enforce the law, and penalties for its violation. After 6 months to a year, have a child try to purchase cigarettes in town from both machines and people. When DiFranza, Norwood, Garner, & Tye (1987) did this in central Massachusetts with an 11-year-old girl, he found that she was able to purchase cigarettes from 86% of the machines and 63% of the cashiers. . . .

Other sections of the strategy memo might include:

- Have other communities or organizations attempted to do the same type of thing you are trying to do? How and where have they been successful? Where and why have they failed? Are there people (either fellow researchers or communications consultants) who have been through this who might be able to help you?
- How widespread should your efforts be? Describe the political or legislative process for obtaining your objective.
- Describe the positive and negative implications of trying to achieve your goal.

What will be the predictable costs and benefits if you succeed? What are the predictable costs and benefits if you fail? Although this type of preparation may appear intimidating at first, it can save a tremendous amount of work and money in the long run by allowing advocates to maintain an efficient and rational course, and by anticipating problems before they occur.

Creating a Communications Campaign

There are times when aiming for exposure in newspapers and on news broadcasts is insufficient or inappropriate. Although limited and irregular communication through news stories may be enough to change the behavior (including the voting behavior) of some individuals, other situations call for both more control over content and repeated exposure to information. This usually means an ongoing campaign that combines exposure through the news with purchased advertising time and space, collateral print materials, and other media.

Typically, intervention programs that attempt such a campaign do so by working with an advertising or public relations agency. Although such agencies offer their services to a limited number of campaigns on a pro bono basis, many organizations who have dealt with them walked away from such allegedly cooperative projects disappointed. A frequent underlying theme in such unsatisfactory relationships is the differing and occasionally opposing goals of the advocates and the advertising agency or public relations firm.

In addition to the sincere desire to do good, one reason these firms do pro bono work is to build recognition within their industry by winning awards. Another is to provide copywriters, art directors, and others with a chance to be "more creative" with a public service account as a reward for their work on more mundane issues.

Unfortunately, such "creativity" sometimes turns into an end to itself, with the behavioral goals of the underlying campaign being forgotten. My favorite extreme example of this was a public service advertisement I saw in the New York City subways in the 1960s. The main text was something like, "Illiterate? Write for help!" followed by an address to which nonreaders would ostensibly write. Clearly, no one in the process thought the problem through.

Although the expertise and experience of advertising and public relations consultants can help a campaign a great deal, it is important that psychologists and other advocates not leap into such relationships simply because those services are offered for free or at a reduced cost. Maintaining a focus on behavioral goals for the intended audience is critical to keeping such cooperative work on track and effective.

Teenage alcohol consumption presents the type of challenge to which psychologists can offer a great deal in the design and implementation stages of a communications campaign. I will use it along with other public health problems in my examples. For the purposes of this chapter, I have chosen to describe the steps to be taken for a well-funded, major campaign. Bear in mind that not all communications campaigns on these types of issues need be this complex or expensive.

A key reason commonly cited for the limited success of most mass media health communications campaigns is inadequate research input at the preparation, production, and dissemination stages of the campaign (Atkin & Freimuth, 1989). Flay and Burton (1990) and Resnick (1990) point out that marketers of retail products allocate substantial resources to research before launching those products, and suggest that public health campaign researchers follow that example if they wish to meet with success.

A poorly designed or targeted campaign may actually increase alcohol problems, doing more harm than good (Moskowitz, 1989). For example, images from designated-driver television campaigns have sometimes modeled heavy drinking by the driver's passengers (DeJong

& Wallack, 1992). Also, other unintended negative effects that could logically result from the campaign (e.g., an antialcohol program leading to increased use of illicit drugs) should be considered and explored (Flay & Petraitis, 1991).

Any communications campaign should begin with both a needs assessment and a theoretical basis for the decisions made in executing the campaign. Campaign designers need a thorough understanding of the problem to be addressed. Social and biological causes of teenage drinking, its relationship to other issues, and its prevalence among subgroups should be researched or reviewed. The theory or theories chosen (e.g., diffusion of innovations, social cognitive theory, theory of reasoned action) will affect the overall design of the campaign as well as message structure and content (Flay & Burton, 1990).

Many campaigns use a traditional persuasion-based framework when designing and testing media messages. Atkin & Freimuth (1989) have condensed those models into five steps:

- exposure to the message (including attention),
- processing message information (including comprehension, selective perception, and evaluation of content),
- cognitive learning (including knowledge and skills acquisition),
- yielding (including the formation or change of beliefs, attitudes, values and intentions), and
- utilization (including retrieving and performing new behaviors, postbehavior consolidation, and long-term continuation).

This model may have limited utility for complex health behaviors; it assumes that the behavior is logically determined and that behavior change follows changes in attitudes and other affective orientations. Not all issues may be suited to traditional persuasive appeals aimed at logical thought processes. There may be situations in which too much information is counterproductive (e.g., if a campaign to increase organ donation dwells too much on the complexities of brain death, or the use of animal organs in transplant, it may result in confusion or negative images that counteract other messages).

Also, as Wallack (1981) pointed out, research has indicated that attitude and behavior change and formation may be affected by different variables, and that attitude change may follow behavior change rather than the reverse. Moskowitz (1989) notes that mass media campaigns on alcohol, like most other health campaigns, are most likely to influence knowledge and least likely to change behavior. Increases in knowledge frequently are found without any corresponding change in either attitudes or behavior (e.g., Collins & Cellucci, 1991).

Flay (1981) suggested that the appropriateness of a behavior-change model depends in part on how involved in or concerned about the issue the target audience is at the start of the campaign, and how different the behavioral alternatives are (e.g., choosing between brands of shampoo is quite different from choosing drinking behaviors).

As Bettinghaus (1988) implied, a review of the design and effects of previous campaigns on similar or related issues (as well as nonpublic health materials, such as television commercials for alcohol), or which have been aimed at similar audiences, is also wise before beginning a campaign. Such a review will help you to avoid repeating mistakes, particularly if detailed information on any formative or summative research is available.

Once the needs assessment and theoretical foundation are in place (or nearly so), formative research can begin. Formative research involves identifying and selecting target audiences, target behaviors and intermediate response (or mediating) variables, media channels used by the target audiences, and audience receptivity to components of potential messages and materials (Atkin & Freimuth, 1989).

Target audiences may be chosen because they are at highest risk for the problem of concern, they have interpersonal influence over a high-risk group, or they are susceptible to media persuasion or influence related to the problem (Atkin & Freimuth, 1989). Media gatekeepers or policymakers are other potential target audiences.

Audiences may be segmented into relatively homogeneous clusters by demographics, behaviors, or other variables for more specific targeting (Flora, Maccoby, & Farquhar, 1989). For example, when Worden and colleagues (1988) conducted formative research for an antismoking media campaign, they knew from prior research that the most common age range in which children began smoking cigarettes was between 10 and 15 years old. They further segmented that group by school grade, designing separate materials appropriate to three different developmental levels (and later, targeting them by gender).

Target behaviors are chosen on the basis of how much they contribute to (or might subtract from) the problem, and how amenable they are to change, particularly through mass media messages (Atkin & Freimuth, 1989). For example, the campaign by Worden and colleagues (1988) focused in part on modeling cigarette refusal skills.

It is also useful to determine the social and environmental factors that affect the target behaviors, and whether and how they are potentially changeable through media or other methods (Atkin & Freimuth, 1989). Campaign content that encourages interpersonal communication about the problem, or mobilization of community resources (e.g., making appealing nonalcoholic beverages more available to college students) may also add to the effectiveness of the campaign (Flay, 1981).

Intermediate responses include those personal factors that encourage or inhibit the desired behavior; for example, lack of awareness of the problem, lack of information or misinformation, dysfunctional attitudes, values, beliefs and images, need for new or clarified terminology, perceived personal relevance of the issue or behavior (especially in the here-and-now) and motivation to change, skills needed to carry out the behavior, and confidence in the ability to perform the behavior as needed (self-efficacy). Some audiences may need their awareness increased, whereas others may already be aware and motivated to change, but lacking in skills or a sense of efficacy (Atkin & Freimuth, 1989; Flora, Maccoby, & Farquhar, 1989).

Similar factors, like perceived social norms or changes in behavioral intentions, when part of a theoretical model, have been termed mediating variables. Such variables must be changed for the ultimate behaviors of concern to be changed. They therefore become a focus of campaign messages (Flay & Petraitis, 1991).

Bauman and colleagues (1988) detailed the formative research process of three antismoking mass media campaigns targeting 12- to 15-year-olds. The first campaign focused on the expected positive and negative social and personal consequences of smoking among ninth graders. The 52 possible consequences were narrowed, through multivariate analysis, to identify the seven most useful in predicting which nonsmokers became smokers one year later. Message design and testing then focused on altering currently nonsmoking young adolescents' expectations of the consequences of smoking.

It is also useful to consider what, if any, needs are being met directly or indirectly through the target audience's current undesirable behavior, and what less-harmful behaviors could be substituted. For example, if smoking cigarettes makes young adolescents feel older, other means of meeting this need can be modeled in messages (and the connection of perceived maturity to smoking can be targeted as well).

Media campaign designers should find out which media channels (e.g., television, radio, magazines), which types of media (e.g., television news, fashion magazines, rock music stations), and which specific media vehicles (e.g., names of magazines and sections read, and television programs viewed) are used and preferred by the target audience. It is also useful to find out how much time they spend using these media, how much attention is generally given to various types of media content, and how credible various channels and programs are. In addition, researchers should explore what secondary channels (e.g., posters, billboards, or direct mail) might be useful to reinforce the mass media messages (Atkin & Freimuth, 1989).

Campaign designers may also develop profiles of potentially relevant media outlets, including ownership, personnel, and program formats (Flora, Maccoby, & Farquhar, 1989). If a partnership with certain media outlets is desired, designers and advocates can seek information on key people and their interests (e.g., the owner, station manager, or news director of a station, or one of their close relatives, may have been treated for a drinking problem; this could translate into support for a campaign to reduce binge drinking among youth).

Designers need to determine what media content the target audience has been or may be exposed to that would contradict or support the campaign messages (e.g., magazine advertisements, movie or entertainment television portrayals, news stories), as well as the kinds of interpersonal communication that have taken place about the issue, and with whom (Atkin & Freimuth, 1989).

It is also helpful to know what kinds of exposure to previous health communications campaigns occurred, particularly related to the problem of concern, and how they were regarded. For example, were such messages paid attention to, was the content memorable, and were they credible? (Atkin & Freimuth, 1989).

One concern is that a clear separation of public service announcements or other prohealth material from all other media content could reduce their potential effectiveness; their known intent to be "good for you" could make them less credible. For example, Worden and colleagues (1988) avoided using a common theme or identifying symbol for the variety of messages they produced, to avoid having teenage viewers "turned off" by associating the messages with an authority source. Rather, the messages appeared to come from a range of sources from the more credible "outside world" of entertainment television—perhaps enhancing the view that smoking was not normative behavior.

In the early phases of the campaign design, the credibility and projected effectiveness of people, themes, persuasive appeals, word choices, music, and stylistic devices or images that might appear in campaign materials should be tested on members of the target audience. As the project advances, message concepts (e.g., rough images, such as storyboards, and key phrases that impart the main content of a proposed message) can also be tested and compared (Atkin & Freimuth, 1989).

For example, Bauman and colleagues (1988) showed still photos of several young actors of different races and genders, dressed in five different types of clothing styles, and asked junior high school classes to rate them on a scale of one to ten (the authors did not note by what criteria). Researchers also asked the students whether, if they wanted to smoke a cigarette, the person in the picture would be able to convince them not to. The process was repeated with focus groups.

One problem with testing message elements in this way is that the effectiveness of a mass media message may depend on the degree to which it models desired new behaviors (Bettinghaus, 1988). This can be hard to determine by testing rough messages in pieces (e.g., when still pictures are used instead of moving, talking actors to assess the potential effects of television messages).

If the campaign designers are working with an outside advertising, public relations, or media consulting company, problems can also result when the outside creative team producing the messages fails to receive, understand, or apply the results of research. To guide message development, Worden and colleagues (1988) produced *Writer's Notebooks*, roughly 125 pages in length, that contained guidelines, audience profiles, sample message concepts, selected comments from focus groups of target audience members, and data tables.

Atkin & Freimuth (1989) suggested that those concepts and elements showing the most promise be put together in rough form (e.g., a photo-based approximation of a television public service announcement or commercial, or a live-action version taped with an inexpensive video recorder), with any music or sound effects included. The goal is to see how the material moves the audience through the hypothesized process of change.

Researchers may assess the ability of the message to hold attention (e.g., asking an audience to recall the content of all messages seen during a "theater test," or watching the eye movements of a small number of TV viewers); comprehensibility of the key messages (including any confusing elements—measured by closed-ended or open-ended questions); whether the message is seen as personally relevant for the target audience (e.g., whether it is "talking to someone like me"); and whether any elements of the message might be inappropriately offensive or controversial (e.g., a breast self-exam message that shows a nude torso).

For example, Bauman and colleagues (1988) taped a sample commercial featuring a close-up shot of a young actress talking about her reaction to seeing a boy she liked smoking. The commercial was shown to single-sex focus groups, embedded in a tape including music videos and two product commercials. Viewers were asked to write down what they remembered about any of the three commercials. They were then asked to discuss, among other issues, what they liked and disliked about the test message (including the actress and her behavior and tone), whether it was boring or interesting, how old they perceived the actress to be, and whether they had learned something from the commercial. Later, the prototype commercial was compared with an expensively produced antismoking advertisement featuring music and dancing, obtained from another source.

Written materials mailed to homes, curriculum materials for schools, worksites or community groups, and discussion of media content by teachers or other influential people are a few of the ways that mass media campaigns can be supplemented or mediated (Bettinghaus, 1988). Print materials, videotapes, or other supplementary materials used also should go through the formative research process described above. Print materials should undergo readability testing to be sure the reading level is appropriate for and comprehensible to the target audience (Arkin, 1989).

Conclusion

The strategies and techniques outlined in this chapter may seem intimidating. Although not all dissemination strategies require the depth of preparation and analysis presented here, the underlying issues should still be addressed in even the smallest communications effort or campaign. Psychologists are particularly qualified to conduct or supervise such efforts. Using our skills and training in this way will significantly increase the effectiveness of our attempts to educate the public and influence public policy through the mass media.

REFERENCES

Arkin, E. B. (1989). *Making health communications programs work: A planner's guide.* Washington, DC: U.S. Dept. of Health and Human Services. (NIH pub. no. 89–1493)

Atkin, C. K., & Freimuth, V. (1989). Formative evaluation research in campaign design. In R. E. Rice & C. K. Atkin (Eds.), *Public communications campaigns* (2nd ed., pp. 131–150). Newbury Park, CA: Sage.

Bauman, K. E., Brown, J. D., Bryan, E. S., Fisher, L. A., Padgett, C. A., & Sweeney, J. M. (1988). Three mass media campaigns to prevent adolescent cigarette smoking. *Preventive Medicine, 17*, 510–530.

Bettinghaus, E. P. (1988). Using the mass media in smoking prevention and cessation programs: An introduction to five studies. *Preventive Medicine, 17*, 503–509.

Buckley, K. W. (1989). *Mechanical man: John Broadus Watson and the beginnings of behaviorism.* New York: Guilford Press.

Collins, D., & Cellucci, T. (1991). Effects of a school-based alcohol education program with a media prevention component. *Psychological Reports*, 191–197.

DeJong, W., & Wallack, L. (1992). The role of designated driver programs in the prevention of alcohol-impaired driving. *Health Education Quarterly, 19*(4), 429–442.

DiFranza, J. R., Norwood, B. D., Garner, D. W., & Tye, J. B. (1987). Legislative efforts to protect children from tobacco. *Journal of the American Medical Association, 257*, 3387–3389.

Fischer, P. M., Schwartz, M. P., Richards, J. W., Goldstein, A. O., & Rojas, T. H. (1991). Brand logo recognition by children aged 3 to 6 years: Mickey Mouse and Old Joe the camel. *Journal of the American Medical Association, 266*, 3145–3148.

Flay, B. R. (1981). On improving the chances of mass media health promotion programs causing meaningful changes in behavior. In M. Meyer (Ed.), *Health education by television and radio* (pp. 57–91). Munich, Germany: Saur.

Flay, B. R., & Burton, D. (1990). Effective mass communication strategies for health campaigns. In C. Atkin & L. Wallack (Eds.), *Mass communication and public health* (pp. 129–146). Newbury Park, CA: Sage.

Flay, B. R., & Petraitis, J. (1991). *Methodological issues in drug use prevention research: Theoretical foundations.* (NIDA Research Monograph 107, 81–109). Washington, DC: U.S. Government Printing Office.

Flora, J. A., Maccoby, N., & Farquhar, W. (1989). Communication campaigns to prevent cardiovascular disease: The Stanford Community Studies. In R. E. Rice & C. K. Atkin (Eds.), *Public communications campaigns* (pp. 233–252). Newbury Park, CA: Sage.

Fox, J. A., & Levin, J. (1993). *How to work with the media.* Newbury Park, CA: Sage.

Kutner, L. A., & Olson, C. K. (1995). *The health professional's guerrilla guide to mass media interviews.* New York: Kutner, Olson & Associates, Inc.

Moskowitz, J. M. (1989). The primary prevention of alcohol problems: A critical review of the research literature. *Journal of Studies on Alcohol, 50*(1), 54–88.

Resnick, M. D. (1990). Study group report on the impact of televised drinking and alcohol advertising on youth. *Journal of Adolescent Health Care, 11*, 25–30.

Schwartz, T. (1973). *The responsive chord.* Garden City, NY: Anchor Press.

Schwartz, T. (1983). *Media: The second god.* Garden City, NY: Anchor Press.

Tobey, J. A. (1925). *The Children's Bureau: Its history, activities and organization.* Baltimore: Johns Hopkins Press.

Wallack, L. M. (1981). Mass media campaigns: The odds against finding behavior change. *Health Education Quarterly, 8,* 209–261.

Wallack, L. M., Dorfman, L., Jernigan, D., & Themba, M. (1993). *Media advocacy and public health.* Newbury Park, CA: Sage.

Watson, J. B. (1928). *Psychological care of infant and child.* New York: Norton.

Wintemute, G., Teret, S., Kraus, J., Wright, M., & Bradfield, G. (1987) When children shoot children: 88 unintended deaths in California. *Journal of the American Medical Association, 257,* 3107–3109.

Worden, J. K., Flynn, B. S., Geller, B. M., Chen, M., Shelton, L. G., Secker-Walker, R. H., Solomon, D. S., Solomon, L. J., Couchey, S., & Costanza, M. C. (1988). Development of a smoking prevention mass media program using diagnostic and formative research. *Preventive Medicine, 17,* 531–558.

Epilogue

Future Directions
for Media Psychology

Sam Kirschner and Diana Adile Kirschner

The field of media psychology has come a long way in terms of its evolution and diversification. This volume chronicles the metamorphosis of practice that began in the days of John B. Watson, who was the media guru of the early twentieth century, continued through the work of the "pioneers" of media psychology, and evolved into the daily contributions of psychologists to the radio, TV, film, and print media in the 1990s.

Not only has the practice of media psychology been transformed in the late twentieth century, but so has the research on the impact of the media on society. This volume contains seminal contributions by the most prominent scholars in the field of media psychology research and includes analyses of the role of television in the lives of children, adolescents, and adults. These studies show how powerfully television impacts on all of us from the time we are toddlers to senior adulthood.

Specifically, they illustrate how this medium shapes people's ability to empathize, and their perceptions of, and attitudes toward, violence, gender, feminism, and aging. These chapters will form a base of information from which future media psychology scholars will draw a wealth of knowledge.

Future media psychologists will also have the benefit of the legitimacy and institutional support of the American Psychological Association (APA). No longer looking askance at media psychology and its practitioners, APA has developed three permanent communications and public relations departments—the Public Information Committee (PIC), the Public Communications Office, and the public relations office of the Practice Directorate. It also has a Media Referral service which offers the names of qualified psychologists who can be interviewed by the print, radio, and TV media. This service has amplified the media presence of virtually every author involved in this volume. And a key APA Division, that of Media Psychology, continues to promote media psychology both within APA and in the public domain.

We would predict, however, that the biggest influx of media psychology work will occur via the staggering technological advances that are going on at this time. As many of the authors in this volume have stated, the biggest revolution will come with these advances. Some of these include digital signal processing, laser technologies, digital video, and fiber and satellite applications. Research will need to focus on the new dimensions of human–machine interactions, specifically on cognitive and emotional reactions to varied and new stimuli.

New technologies, including multimedia, interactive, and virtual reality products, will open other doors for media psychologists. The APA Division of Media Psychology is invested in developing these ripe new areas and will be networking with producers of multimedia and interactive products in order to encourage them to use psychologists in the development of these products. Virtual reality offers a whole new frontier for psychological treatment and research, and we would guess that these types of technological tools will form only a part of a vast armamentarium for future psychologists to use in their work.

We are entering an era of free global telecommunications. Psychologists will be able to make their work cutting edge, as they obtain more and more information regarding current assessment and treatment modalities, strategies and techniques, relevant research findings, strategies or hypotheses, or educational and industrial psychology tools via the use of E-mail and the Internet. A mailing list for "mental-health-in-the-media" already exists, and the Media Psychology Division will soon start its own Media Forum on the World Wide Web.

Over time such connections will allow media psychologists from all over the world to group together and empower themselves. They will be able to collaborate on research and other projects, and they will be able to organize media campaigns on relevant and important issues. As the current trend of acceptance continues over time, more and more psychologists and other mental health professionals will be involved. This will include those working in the clinical and applied areas as well as those working in research.

As media psychology blossoms, its impact should become more and more powerful. This has already been the case: witness the development of the V chip, or Violence chip, which allows parents to control the content of what their children are watching on TV. The V chip came about as political pressures mounted on TV producers to limit the amount of violence in their programming. This legislative pressure arose out of a growing public awareness promoted by 20 years of research on the adverse impact of TV violence on child development (see Donnerstein & Smith, chapter 2, this volume).

Another positive development has emerged from the growing awareness of the impact of television programming on children. This summer President Clinton has forged an agreement whereby broadcasters have agreed to air at least three hours per week of quality children's programming. "We can work to imagine television as a force for good," said President Clinton (Seplow, 1996). Public interest groups will monitor the programming and they have the right to challenge the license renewal of any station that is not in compliance.

Additionally, the Institute for Mental Health Initiatives (IMHI), based in Washington, DC, is built on knowledge grounded by research findings that show that the behavior of characters on television and in film, print media, and music videos has a powerful impact on viewers. Its goal is to transform mental health concepts into positive models of human interaction (IMHI). The Institute has developed workshops, conferences, awards, public service campaigns, and newsletters for the public and key figures in the creative community. Over time, we would anticipate that more groups like this will develop—both within and outside of the American Psychological Association—all designed to promote the public welfare.

The lofty beginning goals of the early media psychologists were to give psychology away to the individual in the mass audience and to promote the profession in the eyes of the public. In the future we will not only expand these goals, we will also actively help to shape our culture by using knowledge to protect and serve the public in a larger and grander way.

REFERENCES

Institute for Mental Health Initiatives. (1996). Language, Sex, Violence, Children. *Dialogue, 4*(3), 1–4. Washington, DC: Author.

Seplow, S. (1996, July 30). Deal struck on children's quality TV. *The Philadelphia Inquirer*, p. 1.

Index

About the Editors

Sam Kirschner, PhD, and **Diana Adile Kirschner,** PhD, are internationally recognized psychologists, seminar leaders, and consultants. They have appeared on numerous TV shows, including "Donahue," "Good Morning America," and "Oprah Winfrey," to discuss psychological, marital, and family issues. The Kirschners have been widely quoted in publications such as the *New York Times, USA Today,* and the *Los Angeles Times,* and in magazines such as *Life* and *Cosmopolitan.* They have co-authored several books, as well as numerous articles and book chapters.

Sam has served as a faculty member of the Wharton School, Division of Family Business Studies and maintains an active consulting practice with both closely held and non-family businesses and corporations.

Diana has also served as a faculty member of the Wharton School, as a task force committee leader for the board of the American Psychological Association (APA) Division of Media Psychology, and on the board of the APA Division of Family Psychology.